Tort Reform by Contract

Tort Reform by Contract
Paul H. Rubin

The AEI Press

Publisher for the American Enterprise Institute
WASHINGTON, D.C.

1993

The author would like to thank Christopher DeMuth for suggesting this book, Clark Havighurst and Jeffrey O'Connell for helpful discussions of the state of the law, and Gregory Sidak and participants at a seminar at AEI for helpful suggestions. The author is responsible for any errors.

The research, writing, and publication of this book were supported by the Paul Oreffice Fund for Legal and Governmental Studies, American Enterprise Institute for Public Policy Research.

Distributed by arrangement with

UPA, Inc.
4720 Boston Way   3 Henrietta Street
Lanham, Md. 20706   London WC2E 8LU England

Library of Congress Cataloging-in-Publication Data
  Tort reform by contract / Paul H. Rubin.
    p. cm.
  Includes bibliographical references.
  ISBN 0-8447-3829-8. — ISBN 0-8447-3828-X (pbk.)
    1. Torts—United States. 2. Law reform—United States.
  3. Contracts—United States. I. Title.
  KF1251.R83 1993
  346.7303—dc20
  [347.3063]
                                                    92-38918
                                                        CIP

    1 3 5 7 9 10 8 6 4 2

Printed in the United States of America

Contents

vi

Foreword

Legal liability for accidents has expanded considerably in recent decades as courts have revised traditional legal standards of causation, liability, evidence, and damages in accident lawsuits. Newspaper reports of huge damage awards (often greatly exceeding the actual costs of medical treatment and lost income resulting from an injury) against business firms and providers of medical and other services have become commonplace, as have reports of firms declining to market potentially valuable products and of physicians practicing costly "defensive medicine" in response to liability concerns. These developments have led to boisterous political debates in Congress and state legislatures—generally pitting producer groups against trial lawyers—over tort reform bills aimed at restoring previous legal standards by statute.

The political debates have been reflected in more austere but equally contentious debates among legal scholars. Some academic students of the liability system argue that a liability explosion is indeed imposing fabulous costs on the American economy—retarding innovation, increasing costs to consumers, and damaging U.S. competitiveness with other nations that maintain more reasonable accident liability regimes. Others assert that recent modifications of legal standards have been, at least for the most part, beneficial responses to modern economic developments (such as increased division of labor and specialization of knowledge, and increased income, wealth, and aversion to risk). Additional arguments are that the popular perception of a liability explosion is exaggerated (focusing, for example, on dramatic jury awards that are later overturned or modified by trial or appellate judges) and that, even if the liability explosion is real and harmful, it is no worse than the cure of legislating—and thereby to some degree politicizing—accident law.

This volume introduces a new argument, of great potential significance, to both the political and the academic debates over accident liability. Paul H. Rubin asks us to set aside questions of appropriate standards of liability (that determine when the costs of an injury will be assessed against another party) and to focus on the types of costs assessed when courts do impose liability. He demonstrates that "high" damages—damages exceeding an injured party's tangible, pecuniary costs of medical care and lost income—are of little value to consumers and not worth their actuarial cost before an accident. Although this demonstration is made theoretically, the basic point may be grasped by observing that individuals generally purchase (that is, are willing to pay the costs of) insurance for their own medical expenses and lost wages in the event of illness or injury but virtually never purchase insurance for pain and suffering, lost companionship, and related intangible losses customarily assessed by courts in accident cases.

Judicial award of "high" damages—which are a cost of production and go into the prices of goods and services that may involve injuries—effectively obliges consumers to pay for a form of insurance that they would rather do without. And therefore—coming finally to Professor Rubin's reform proposal summarized in the title of this volume—courts should allow producers and consumers to specify in advance the extent of damages to be paid in the event of an accident. If courts enforced such contractual specifications, goods and services involving potential injury would generally be sold subject to a limitation of damages (in the event of the seller's liability for an accident) to pecuniary damages for medical care, lost income, and related tangible losses: it is only these sorts of losses that consumers are generally willing to insure against. This result depends on no unrealistic assumptions about producers and consumers negotiating over the terms of individual sales and services. In competitive markets, goods and services sold with damage limitations—at lower prices reflecting the savings in "high" damage payments—would take business from identical goods and services offered without damage limitations.

Such damage limitations are extremely rare today because courts do not enforce them. Once an accident has occurred, the injured party naturally seeks the highest possible damage award, regardless of any preaccident agreement. In response to such pleas, courts have fashioned a number of rationales for refusing to enforce damage-limitation contracts in accident cases—usually in the belief that this refusal protects consumers, a belief Professor Rubin shows is not only mistaken but backward. There are, however, some useful precedents at hand; for example, damage limitations involving losses other than personal injuries, such as the familiar limitation on the side of a box of photographic film, are routinely enforced. Professor Rubin argues forcefully that expanding these precedents to embrace cases of accident liability would benefit producers and consumers alike and, indeed, would be likely to lead to safer products and services and fewer accidents.

Although Professor Rubin describes his proposal as "modest," it would, if adopted by courts or legislatures, go a considerable way toward solving the problems of our accident liability system, whatever their magnitude. The "high," nonpecuniary damages that would generally be excluded under his proposal have come to be a substantial portion of total damages awarded in liability cases and have undoubtedly added a bonanza potential to tort litigation that has compromised its social role of minimizing the incidence and costs of accidents.

One does not need to take sides in either the political or the academic debates over the liability explosion to see the virtue of Professor Rubin's approach. His proposal, moreover, does not depend on legislation and may proceed incrementally through case-by-case development in the courts. For these reasons as well as for its intrinsic interest, Professor Rubin's study merits careful consideration by judges and practicing attorneys as well as those directly engaged in the liability reform debates.

CHRISTOPHER C. DEMUTH
President, American Enterprise Institute
for Public Policy Research

About the Author

Paul H. Rubin is professor of economics at Emory University. He has taught economics at the University of Georgia, City University of New York, Virginia Polytechnic Institute, and George Washington University Law School.

Professor Rubin has been chief economist, U.S. Consumer Product Safety Commission; senior advertising economist, Federal Trade Commission; senior staff economist, President Ronald Reagan's Council of Economic Advisers; and vice president, Glassman-Oliver Economic Consultants, with which he is still affiliated.

He is a frequent contributor to the *Wall Street Journal* and has published in the *American Economic Review*, *Journal of Political Economy*, *Quarterly Journal of Economics*, *Journal of Legal Studies*, and *Journal of Law and Economics*. Professor Rubin's books include *Congressmen, Constituents, and Contributors* (1982), with James B. Kau; *Business Firms and the Common Law* (1983); and *Managing Business Transactions: Controlling the Costs of Coordinating, Communicating, and Decision Making* (1990).

He earned a BA from the University of Cincinnati and a PhD in economics from Purdue University. Professor Rubin is an adjunct scholar at the American Enterprise Institute and the Cato Institute.

1
Introduction

Accidents occur in two types of situations. In one type, the injurer and the victim are strangers: they have no prior relationship with each other. An example is the typical automobile accident.

In the second type, the two parties have some relationship before the injury. A patient purchases services from a physician before malpractice occurs; a consumer buys a product before any harm leads to a product liability suit; a worker accepts a job with an employer before an injury happens.

Until fairly recently, the legal system has treated these two types of accidents differently. Historically, the first type of accidents was the province of tort law, the law governing accidents between strangers. The second was more nearly the province of contract law. With contracts, the parties could specify the terms governing a mishap. Often these terms were specified in the warranty associated with a product or service. Warranties, for example, commonly disclaimed any responsibility of the manufacturer for consequential damages, damages arising from the failure of the product over and above the value of the product itself. (If a refrigerator breaks, the cost of the food that spoils is a consequential damage. Injuries associated with the use of a product are also a form of consequential damages.)

In recent years, this distinction has been virtually eliminated by the court system. The beginning of the fundamental revolution replacing contract by tort dates to two cases decided in the 1960s.[1] These cases eliminated privity (a contractual term limiting damage payments to direct purchasers of a product) and established strict

---

[1] Henningsen v. Bloomfield Motors, 32 N.J. 358, 161 A.2d 69 (1960), and Greenman v. Yuba Power Products Co., 59 Cal. 2d 57, 377 P.2d 897, 27 Cal. Rptr. 697 (1963).

liability for product-related injuries, even if the parties had specified another standard for liability. The courts are now unwilling to accept contractual limits in injury cases with a prior relationship between the injurer and the injured. This unwillingness may apply both to standards of liability and to limits of damage payments. That is, the courts apply something approximating strict liability to product injury cases, no matter what standard the parties desire, and the courts may determine damage payments independently of any contractual specification of payments. Indeed, since the courts appear not to accept such contractual limitations, parties seldom bother to write them. But, as shown later, courts might accept damage payment limiting contracts if parties did write such contracts.

George L. Priest (1985) has written an excellent intellectual history of modern product liability law. The basic impetus for the change from contract to tort came from the work of Fleming James and Friedrich Kessler. James believed that tort law should serve to provide insurance by spreading risk. Kessler believed that contracts did not truly reflect the wishes of the parties since many contracts were not freely negotiated (so-called contracts of adhesion) and since businesses and consumers had unequal bargaining power. We will see below that product liability law is an ineffective method of risk spreading, so that James's arguments are incorrect, and that the concept of contracts of adhesion is not helpful in understanding contracts in an economic setting. In other words, both intellectual pillars of modern product liability law are defective.

Scholars of tort law disagree about the wisdom of replacing contract by tort. William Landes and Richard Posner (1987), Steven Shavell (1987), and Stephen P. Croley and Jon D. Hansen (1991), writing in a law and economics tradition, believe that this change is desirable.[2] Richard A. Epstein (1985), Jules L. Coleman (1989), John Calfee and Paul Rubin (1992), Patricia Danzon (1985), Clark C. Havighurst (1986), Peter W. Huber (1988), Alan Schwartz (1988), and Priest (1987), among others, believe that the change is undesirable. These latter scholars would probably endorse many or all of the arguments made here; indeed, many have made similar points. The proposal in this work, however, while advocating a partial return to contract, is not inconsistent with the arguments of Landes and Posner

---

[2]This view would be much more prevalent among conventional legal torts scholars.

and of Shavell (although they do not directly address the issues raised here).

In the following analysis, I address the issue of contractual specification of damage payments or rules for determining damage payments. The analysis applies equally to product liability, medical malpractice, and workplace injuries, because, in all three cases, parties are in a position to agree on terms before the mishap. (I generally refer to products, but the analysis is more general.) I do not directly address the issue of liability rules.

Basic Arguments

In this work, I make three major, related arguments:

1.   When potential injurers and potential victims have a contractual relationship with each other, they should be permitted to specify contractually the level or type of damages that will be paid if an accident occurs.

2.   If such contracts were allowed, then parties would choose to limit possible damage payments. Some types of damage payments that the courts now award would be eliminated by contract if the parties could contract to do so. The types of damage payments they would eliminate are predictable, and the decision to eliminate these payments is consistent with rational behavior by consumers.

3.   If such contracts were allowed, then many of the problems ascribed to the tort system would be solved.

Contractual Specification of Damage Payments. Current policy, which does not allow contractual specification of damage payments for injury, is in error. Courts should allow parties to specify by contract the allowable damage payments for an accident, and parties should specify damage payments in contracts. The argument here is based on showing that parties to contracts of the sort at issue here would prefer limits on damage awards.

This preference may be obvious for potential injurers: they would naturally prefer smaller damage payments if they are sued and lose. Less obviously, potential victims would also prefer to contract for smaller damage payments before an accident. Because injurers and victims have a contractual relationship with each other, victims must

3

pay for any expected damage payments. They pay in the form of higher prices for products or services or through lower wages. The market will lead to increased prices to compensate for any expected damage awards. Consumers place low values on certain types of damage payments and, thus, would not want to pay the expected cost of these payments in the price of the product.

Damage Compensation That Consumers Do and Do Not Desire. Consumers' preferred damage payments are predictable and rational. Some types of losses can be replaced by money payments. When cars or houses are destroyed by fire, consumers can purchase new ones as a replacement, if they have access to enough money. Injured consumers lose wages and may require medical care. Lost wages can be replaced by money; medical care must be paid for. Losses that can be replaced by a payment of money are called pecuniary losses, indicating that they can, in some sense, be monetized. Consumers generally insure against pecuniary losses. Consumers contracting with potential injurers want compensation for possible pecuniary losses.

Other losses cannot be replaced by payment of money. These losses are called nonpecuniary. Pain and suffering is one class of such a loss. The loss to survivors of the pleasure of dealing with a deceased person (called loss of consortium for a deceased spouse in the legal system) is not measurable or compensable in money terms. What is now called the lost pleasure of life is also a nonpecuniary loss. Loss of irreplaceable items with a low monetary value (the family Bible, the family dog) are also nonpecuniary losses. Consumers do not insure against this class of loss (for reasons discussed below), and if consumers could contract with potential injurers, they would elect not to be compensated for this class of harms.

A recent case, *Molzof v. United States*,[3] illustrates these types of losses. Robert Molzof underwent surgery at a Veterans Administration hospital. As a result of uncontested negligence, a respirator and its alarm were disconnected, and Molzof suffered irreversible brain damage. The VA agreed to provide medical care for Molzof for the rest of his life and to pay $75,750 for future medical expenses for care of a sort not provided by the VA hospital; these were payments (in kind and

---

[3]60 U.S.L.W. 4081, January 14, 1992.

in cash) for pecuniary losses. The VA also paid $150,000 to Molzof's wife for loss of consortium, a nonpecuniary loss.

The issues in the case were whether the VA should also pay Molzof for his "lost enjoyment of life," also called hedonic damages (discussed below), and whether it should pay him cash for the amount of his future medical care in addition to actually providing that care. Under the governing statute, the Federal Tort Claims Act, punitive damages (damages assessed to punish defendants for extreme carelessness rather than to compensate plaintiffs for losses) were not allowed; the issue in dispute was whether the duplicated medical expenses and the figures for the lost enjoyment of life constituted punitive damages. While the opinions do not indicate the magnitude of damage payments requested for the lost pleasure of life, usual figures are $2–9 million. The amount asked for future medical care was $1.3 million. The court held that payment for the lost pleasure of life was compensatory rather than punitive but that payment for the value of medical care—duplicating the actual provision of care—was punitive. The requested medical care payment was therefore denied, and the case was remanded to determine if the lost pleasure of life was compensable under Wisconsin law, the governing law in the case. Thus, in this example, nonpecuniary and punitive damage amounts were larger than pecuniary damage payments.

Contractual Specification of Damage Payments as a Solution. The relative dollar amounts in *Molzof* are typical. In general, nonpecuniary damage payments are now about half of total payments (and under some current proposals for legal change, discussed below, would become significantly larger). Eliminating this type of damage payment would greatly reduce direct payments through the tort system. Moreover, by limiting potential returns to plaintiffs and their attorneys from litigation, such a policy would reduce the incentive of potential plaintiffs to bring cases, particularly speculative cases based on new legal theories. Empirical evidence indicates that, for malpractice, limiting damage payments is the reform with the largest effect on premium rates. We would expect similar results with litigation and insurance for general product liability. Thus, a reform that would limit damage payments would also reduce the number of cases brought. Nonpecuniary damages are the least certain and the most difficult to measure. The economic theory of litigation shows that reduction of

5

uncertainty would lead to less litigation and more settlement out of court, again reducing costs.

Plan of the Work

There are several proposals for tort reform in the literature and in policy discussions. One point of this analysis is to present yet another proposal. The proposal here is based in contract, however, with little, if any, need for statutory change. Chapter 2 discusses the advantage of returning to a regime of contracts for product-related injuries. Conversely, some economists argue that the decision by the courts to ignore contracts has been correct; these arguments are discussed and criticized in chapter 3.

Since damage payments ultimately go to victims who are consumers, consumers might be assumed to be indifferent between paying high prices and receiving high damage awards, and paying low prices and receiving low payments. This, however, is not the case. Rather, consumers would prefer not to pay for higher damage compensation. The value of these payments to injured consumers is less than their cost to purchasers, even if the costs are the mathematically fair expected values of the payments. The argument showing this is complex; it is presented in chapter 4, the most technical chapter in the work.

Damage payments perform two functions: (1) they reimburse injured consumers and (2) they provide incentives for potential injurers to take proper care to avoid injury. Most economists believe that the second function is more important than the first. Many argue that large damage payments are needed to provide proper incentives for potential injurers to take care. This argument is based on the flawed assumption that the only mechanism for safety is the tort system. This point is covered in chapter 5, with a discussion of alternative mechanisms for safety, including regulation and reputation.

If the courts do allow parties to contracts to limit damage payments, that would have important policy implications: large damage awards have harmful effects on consumers and on the economy. Chapter 6 discusses some current proposals for *increasing* damage payments (beyond their current level) and shows, in general, the harm generated by large payments, both existing and potential. It points out the benefits that would accrue if courts allow contractual limits for damage payments, if I am correct in arguing that parties would usually choose to limit such payments if they were allowed to.

One benefit of contractual tort reform is that parties may be able to accomplish this reform on their own, independent of the court system and of the legislature. While this is not certain, there is some evidence that courts are beginning to allow such limits on damage payments. Chapter 7 discusses this evidence and provides some suggestions for drafting contracts that are more likely to be accepted by the courts. Chapter 8 provides a summary of the argument of the book.

2
Contractual Remedies to Tort Problems

Readers need no convincing that many authorities believe that current tort and product liability law in the United States has been misguided. Many who believe this have suggested reforms. I also suggest reform. I first indicate the nature of my proposal and briefly explain its advantages. I propose greater reliance on contracts for specifying damage payment amounts. I also discuss a few alternative proposals for tort reform and indicate why I believe my proposal is preferable.

Contractual Specification of Damage Payments

The change in liability law recommended here is simple. Where there is a prior relationship between injurers and victims (product liability, workplace injury, medical malpractice), the parties should be allowed to specify by contract or warranty the types of damages for which injurers will be liable.

This is not a full-blown return to contracts for product liability harms (even though such a return might be desirable). Rather, it is a return to contracts only for one part of the liability equation, albeit an important part. Nonetheless, many aspects of tort law over which parties might like to reach private agreements (for example, strict liability versus negligence, standards of care, privity of contract) are omitted from the analysis.

My proposal is not unique: many others have advocated a return to contract, at least for medical malpractice. Epstein (1986 and elsewhere) and Havighurst (1986) have been strong advocates for a return to contracts. Havighurst indicates that parties might adopt many of the limitations that I also suggest they might prefer, as does Coleman (1989). Schwartz (1988) also advocates a return to contract principles, although his proposal is much more complex. Robert D. Cooter and Stephen D. Sugarman (1988) advocate a market in unmatured tort claims and indicate that this market would operate essentially by reducing the costs of products. Jeffrey O'Connell (1981, 1990) has made similar proposals.

Economic theory indicates that if contracting over damage payments were allowed, then parties might limit the amount of awards that would be allowed. Chapter 4 discusses the theory: I explain why parties would likely choose to limit damage amounts and show which types of damage parties would probably include. At this point, it is sufficient to indicate that such damage payment limitations would be likely. In particular, parties would probably allow damage payments for pecuniary losses (including medical care and some fraction of lost wages) but not for nonpecuniary losses (pain and suffering, emotional distress, lost pleasure of life).

Benefits from the Proposal

There are two major benefits from this limited approach. First, the approach is voluntary. Second, implementation would be relatively easy, at least relative to alternatives in the literature.

Voluntarism. One important benefit of a contractual approach is that it is voluntary. That is, both parties (potential injurer and potential victim) must agree to the limitation before it can be put in place. As indicated, chapter 4 provides a sustained argument regarding the types of damage payments parties would likely agree to. The argument, however, is largely theoretical. We do not currently observe the contractual specification of the type of damage, and, so, we have no data to demonstrate the correctness of the argument. Therefore, the theory might be wrong. Parties might not desire the menu of damage payments that I predict they would desire.

But with a contractual solution, nothing is lost if I am wrong. The costs of any errors are self-limiting. I predict that parties in a voluntary transaction will adopt certain specific terms, but all I propose is that we allow parties to engage in the voluntary transaction. If my predictions are incorrect, the process is self-correcting. Parties will simply not adopt the terms that I suggest. They may opt for even less in the way of damage awards than I suggest. Conversely, they may, in fact, desire the current set of rules; Croley and Hanson (1991) argue that current laws are better than previous doctrines and that consumers benefit from the current regime in tort law. I believe that their argument is mistaken on several counts,[1] but if they are correct and I am wrong, then my approach will cost nothing, because consumers will simply not agree to the terms that I predict.

An Easy Solution. A second benefit of the proposed solution is that it may be relatively easy to implement. Parties can themselves write whatever contracts they desire. We do not need legislation to implement the policies that I am proposing. Rather, they can be put in practice with relatively minor changes in interpretation by the courts. Indeed, since no contracts have been written in the form that I am suggesting, it may be that no decision by the courts is actually needed.

The courts might uphold such contracts, even if there is no statutory change. This is particularly likely because many judges now (at least on the federal bench) appear to believe in principles of contractual freedom. Much of the change in antitrust law in recent years (which has been moving toward relatively more efficient outcomes) has been driven by judicial rulings, rather than by statute, as discussed by William E. Kovacic (1991). The same mechanism may be useful for tort reform as well.

The argument advanced here may make it more likely that the courts will accept agreed on damage payments. I present arguments based on rational individual behavior in favor of certain damage principles. If the parties contract for this level of damages, attorneys for defendants involved in an accident followed by litigation may be able to present convincing arguments as to why parties would have agreed to this level of damage payments. This will provide a sound theoretical alternative to a theory of unequal bargaining power to explain the form of the agreement.

Moreover, there are reasons for believing that the courts might accept this solution. I do not advocate complete elimination of damage

---

[1]They argue, for example, that consumers would want compensation for nonpecuniary losses, but I show in chapter 4 that this is incorrect. This is a key part of their argument, and, in my view, a key mistake. For a thorough critique of their arguments, see Priest 1992.

payments. Rather, the damage amounts to which parties are likely to contract are losses of earnings and medical payments. This measure of damages is roughly equivalent to payments in workmen's compensation cases. Therefore, an argument against finding such contracts unconscionable or against public policy is that this measure of damages has been mandated by statute for a wide class of accidents and, therefore, is not in any sense against the public interest.

I suggest that parties would contract for compensation for actual monetary losses, including medical expenses and lost earnings. If so, injured parties would not be likely to become public charges, and society would not be forced to pay for their treatment or support. Therefore, there would be no argument that the contracts would lead to increased welfare spending or other public costs or that the poor or others lacking in medical insurance would be disadvantaged. Courts could not use these arguments to invalidate the contracts.

Chapter 7 discusses in detail the legal arguments regarding the likely acceptance of such contracts by the courts and the contractual form that would make such acceptance more likely. Even if the courts will not uphold contractual limitations of damage payments, the statutory change needed to obtain this limit may be relatively small. Many states have already passed laws capping damage payments for various types of torts. The proposal here is less interventionist than a cap. Rather than limiting damage payments to a fixed amount determined by legislators, payments can be at whatever level the parties agree to before the accident. It would be odd (but, unfortunately, not impossible) if state legislatures were themselves willing to specify damage payments for injured consumers but not willing to allow consumers to choose their own level of desired damage amounts in situations where choice is possible. The arguments in this book can also be presented to legislators to help convince them that such a statutory change would benefit consumers.

Alternatives

The voluntary nature of my proposal and the ease with which it might be adopted stand in contrast to other proposals in the literature, which are more complex and which would probably require statutory implementation. A review of some typical proposals for reform demonstrates those qualities.

11

Alan Schwartz (1988) presents a well thought-out, well-argued, and well-crafted set of reforms, based on a careful analysis of consumer preferences. Much of the analysis agrees with my proposals; Schwartz argues strongly, for example, that compensation for nonpecuniary losses is undesirable, for essentially the same reasons that I discuss. If legal change were costless, then Schwartz's proposals might be desirable, but these proposals would be much more difficult to implement, and, therefore, are much less likely to be implemented, than my suggestions. Schwartz's proposals are for default rules, rules that govern unless the parties specify different rule contractually. In allowing freedom of contract, his suggestions are identical to mine. I would not, however, go so far in specifying default rules.

Schwartz would reform the liability standard. He suggests a rule of strict liability but with a complete defense of contributory negligence or of assumption of risk. Warnings should be a stronger defense against liability than is now true.

For damage payments for pecuniary losses, Schwartz would hold firms liable. He would, however, allow consumers to pay a low price and to purchase products with no bundled insurance, if the consumer could demonstrate that he had first-party insurance. He argues that courts should not award nonpecuniary damages, but that legislatures should consider a system of fines on firms, with the amounts rebated to consumers, for adequate safety incentives, and that punitive damage payments should be limited to "outrageous" cases.

W. Kip Viscusi (1991) suggests complex reforms that do not rely on contract:[2] use of regulatory agencies rather than tort litigation to determine if products should be manufactured at all; replacement of the current risk-utility test with a negligence standard to determine if additional safety features are justified; improvements in hazard warnings and in doctrine relating to warnings; and use of deterrence (willingness to pay) values when the goal of tort liability is deterrence.

While some of these proposals (return to a negligence standard, improvement of warning labels) are sensible, others are puzzling. Viscusi would rely more heavily on regulatory agencies to determine if products should be sold. He cites, however, thirteen studies of the effects of existing regulation in several contexts (p. 122). Of these studies, only one found unambiguously beneficial effects of regulation,

---

[2]This discussion is based on Rubin 1992.

and two others found possibly beneficial effects. The other ten studies found either no significant beneficial effects or negative effects. Thus, it is not clear why Viscusi thinks that increased reliance on regulatory efforts would be beneficial, given the record of such efforts to date.

Similarly, Viscusi indicates that using deterrence values for damage payments (which I call hedonic values and discuss in chapter 6) would lead to a tenfold increase in payments, but he advocates such policies in some cases. He presents no evidence, however, indicating that juries would be able to determine appropriate cases for such awards. Hence, this policy would likely jack up damage payments, with substantial harmful effects. An analogy may be warnings. While well-designed warnings should enable manufacturers to escape liability, the courts have essentially used warning doctrine to create another possibility for finding liability. In chapter 6, I show that excessive damage payments have detrimental effects on resource allocation through price effects.

The major puzzle about the policies that Viscusi advocates is this: product liability litigation occurs when plaintiffs (consumers) have a pre-accident contractual relationship with defendants (firms). Viscusi himself has been a leader in showing that much risk is by choice in contractual situations. Nowhere in this book does evidence indicate that product risks are excessive—that is, that the level of risks in products is greater than the level that consumers would desire if they could choose. Priest (1985) has shown that the switch from contract to tort in product liability was the result of a misconception by academic lawyers, and Viscusi presents no evidence inconsistent with this argument. Therefore, a natural question to ask is, Why not advocate a return to contracts to control risks associated with products in potential contractual settings? Viscusi does not allude to this reform, but his arguments and data are consistent with the approach suggested here.

The Council on Competitiveness (1991), a federal policy group, wrote a set of guidelines aimed at civil justice reform. The rationale for the proposals indicates that the main concern was tort law. All the proposals require legislation. Moreover, the proposals govern only federal law, a relatively small part of all tort law. Twenty-two recommendations are divided into nine categories: voluntary dispute resolution; discovery; more effective trial procedures; expert evidence reform; punitive damages; improved use of federal judicial resources; enhanced incentives for encouraging meritorious litigation; reducing

13

unnecessary burdens on federal courts; and eliminating litigation over poorly drafted legislation. None of these proposals address nonpecuniary damages, and none address potential contractual issues.

Randall R. Bovberg, Frank A. Sloan, and James F. Blumstein (1989) and Greg Niehaus and Edward A. Snyder (1992) propose scheduling damage payments for pain and suffering; there would be a fixed payment schedule, with the amount of payment for a given type of harm predetermined, much as in workmen's compensation. This proposal is not inconsistent with my argument. If consumers prefer scheduled payments for pain and suffering, then such payments will be made available. As I indicate below, however, consumers would actually prefer no payments for these nonpecuniary losses. A contract solution does not require that we decide this issue; participants in the market will reach their own decision.

Clearly, the proposals advocated here are much simpler than many of the proposals in the literature. While my proposals may have other advantages, their relative simplicity and ease of adoption are a strong argument for them. Moreover, the proposals may be achievable with no legislative reforms, through change only in private contractual terms.

Why Only Damage Payments?

Why limit the proposal to the contractual specification of damage awards? Why not allow contracts to return to the entire class of events associated with product liability law? There are strong arguments to be made for this proposal (for example, Epstein 1986; Danzon 1984; Priest 1985; Huber 1988; Havighurst 1986), and this should be the ultimate goal of reform. There are, however, some theoretical and practical advantages for initially limiting the proposed reform to damage payments. These advantages notwithstanding, the arguments made in this work can be considered as justifying the contractual specification of damages as part of a more comprehensive reform package allowing contractual specification of other parts of tort law. While damage reform is important, the only reason to limit reform to damages is that this reform might be easier to implement. There are several advantages to concentrating initially on damages.

First, there is a greater probability that the courts will accept contracted rules for damage payments than for liability. The principles of law that reject contracted liability rules are quite settled, and precedents are strong. (This issue is discussed in chapter 7.) No precedents deal solely with limitations to damage payments. Therefore, the courts can more easily adopt such contracts, if they so desire.

Second, as mentioned, some states have already adopted caps to damage amount by statute. Limits to damage amounts by contract are less invasive than damage caps: parties are able to choose for themselves the level of damages for an accident. Therefore, it may be easier to get legislative approval of the proposal here than of a more comprehensive proposal, if legislative approval should be required.

Third, the benefits of limiting damage payments in this way may be greater than first appears. As discussed later, a limitation to contracted damage amounts would probably reduce expected payments by about 50 percent. If amounts are reduced by this amount, then the incentive for filing cases is reduced. This effect would particularly apply to cases based on novel theories of liability, since the expected returns to attorneys of such litigation would be reduced by limiting potential damage awards, while the expected costs of litigation would not change.

Evidence from states that have adopted various forms of tort reform indicates that by far the most powerful change for limiting insurance costs is a damage cap. Such caps can lower insurance premiums by about 30 percent (Zuckerman, Bovberg, and Sloan 1990; Blackmon and Zeckhauser 1991). Since I hypothesize that consumers would completely eliminate compensation for pain and suffering, rather than merely capping it, the proposal here would probably lower premiums by even more.

Fourth, the proposals do not directly contradict many academic supporters of current product liability law. My proposal might generate less academic hostility than would other proposals. This argument applies both to economists and noneconomists who have studied tort law.

Among economists, as discussed in chapter 3, theoretical arguments advanced by Landes and Posner (1987) and Shavell (1987) support the movement from contract to tort in product liability matters. I do not accept these arguments, for reasons discussed in chapter 3. Even if they are correct, however, their arguments apply to liability rules but not to damage payments. Therefore, reform limited to damage amounts is less likely to do harm than would be a complete return to contract if Landes and Posner as well as Shavell are correct. Moreover, it may be easier to convince others of the strength of the argument if there are no powerful counterarguments. In addition, as I show more carefully in chapter 3, the proposal here—for contractual specification of damage payments only—is consistent with their analyses.

Consider some noneconomists. Maxwell J. Mehlman (1990) believes that principles of fiduciary law rather than contract should govern product-related accidents. This belief leads to an emphasis on asymmetric information regarding risk probabilities. His argument, however, would not apply to information about desired compensation for whatever injuries did occur. Thus, the proposal here may not be inconsistent with Mehlman's claims. Peter A. Bell (1990) seems somewhat confused on the economic arguments regarding nonpecuniary losses; he argues, for example, that the only saving from contractual specification of damage amounts would be reduced transactions costs (p. 1197). Later, he seems to argue for nonpecuniary damage payments as a form of deterrence, again without understanding the economic analysis (pp. 1232–33). Nonetheless, the heart of his analysis is a discussion of asymmetric information (pp. 1225–29): there is less reason to believe that such lack of understanding would be relevant for damage principles than for liability standards.

Fifth, as we see in chapter 6, there are no good measures of nonpecuniary damages. In general, if there is uncertainty about expected damage payments, then litigation is more probable. Restricting damage awards to pecuniary losses would therefore make damage payments much more predictable. If damage amounts are more certain, then the probability of litigating those cases that are filed will be reduced, and out-of-court settlement will be more likely. This saving in litigation costs will also be a significant benefit of eliminating nonpecuniary losses.

Finally, we may view the reforms suggested here as a first step. If parties do limit payments as I predict and if the courts do honor these contracts, this may be a first step in returning to a more soundly grounded contractual regime. After all, the change from contract to tort was not a single one-step change, and there is no reason to expect the movement back to contract to be a single move either.

Contracts of Adhesion?

Many of the contracts that would result from this proposal would probably be standard form contracts, offered with products; the

16

consumer could not reject the contract without also rejecting the entire transaction. Since the work of Kessler, some have argued that such contracts should be invalid, because consumers are "forced" to accept the contract. The contract is called a contract of adhesion. These same authorities argue that there is unequal bargaining power between consumers and producers and that therefore consumers have no choice but to accept terms offered by firms.

Although this doctrine is pervasive in the legal literature, it makes no sense. Consider price. In a modern retail establishment, a consumer cannot bargain over price; price is a term of adhesion just as much as the terms of the warranty are. Indeed, except for goods made to order, *all* characteristics of goods are adhesion characteristics. We cannot request an automobile in a color that is not made or with an extra-large trunk. We can obtain air bags only if we buy a model that offers this feature. Most of us would have trouble locating a blue and orange polka-dot man's suit, since suits are offered for sale only in colors of adhesion.

Contract terms are no different. Firms can compete over warranties and other terms of the contract, including safety guarantees, just as well as they can compete over any other product characteristic. Indeed, firms do sometimes compete over warranty terms. From time to time, automobile companies have competed over warranty terms. Moreover, it is often possible to buy extended warranties on automobiles or on appliances unbundled from the product itself. If my arguments are wrong and consumers do indeed desire warranties that cover nonpecuniary damages as well as pecuniary losses and if consumers are willing to pay the cost of such warranties, then firms will offer these terms.

It may be true that, if a particular producer does not offer a warranty that a consumer desires, then the consumer cannot buy the product of that producer with that warranty. But this view gives too little play to competition. If the consumer and enough others do want such a contractual feature, then some other producer will find it in his interest to offer the terms, just as producers compete by offering product characteristics that consumers desire. It makes no more sense to regulate contractual terms than to regulate any other terms of private transactions. Moreover, although one consumer may have no bargaining power with an individual producer, if enough consumers desire some feature (contractual or otherwise) then producers can make

17

money by offering this term, and this possibility will lure firms into satisfying consumers' desires, independently of bargaining power.

The arguments in this book explain why consumers might want certain types of contracts associated with potential injuries from products. If these arguments are correct, then firms would offer this type of contract in a world in which contractual freedom was not restricted. If this occurs, then it will be fallacious for courts to invalidate these contracts on the basis that all (or most) firms offered the same terms, so that consumers had little choice. Priest (1981) has shown that most firms offer similar warranty terms, because these warranties are efficient. The same point would apply to damage-limiting contracts. The arguments here suggest that consumers would want certain contracts; if consumers do indeed choose this type of contract, that choice would indicate that the theoretical arguments are correct, not that consumers lack bargaining power.

3
Economic Literature on Contracts and Tort

Many writers in the law and economics tradition have advocated a return to contract principles in product liability litigation (for example, Coleman 1989; Calfee and Rubin 1992; Danzon 1984; Epstein 1984; Havighurst 1986; Priest 1987). Despite these writings, the conventional view in the economics of law literature is that contracts are not desirable for products liability law. The two major treatises on the economics of torts (Landes and Posner 1987; Shavell 1987) disagree on various points, but both argue that contracts are not an efficient solution to risks associated with purchased products. This concept has led Huber, a major critic of modern tort law, to suggest that "legal economists" have provided sophisticated justifications for changes in modern tort law (1988, p.6).[1] (A major textbook in the field, Cooter and Ulen 1988, does indicate that "the older common law, by basing recovery for product-related harms on contract principles through the requirement of privity, may have had strengths that are not generally recognized today" [p. 430].)

The basic argument against contractual solutions for product liability problems is best summarized by Landes and Posner:

> The answer [to the question, Why not a contractual solution?] is that contracts are costly to make and that the costs may well

---

[1]"Arriving on the scene of the great tort battle late in the day, they [the legal economists] courageously congratulated the victors, shot the wounded, and pronounced the day's outcome satisfactory and good." In the set of legal economists, Huber includes Guido Calabresi, Richard Posner, and "many others, for economists seem to be almost as numerous as lawyers."

exceed the benefits, relative to regulation by tort law, when the contingencies that would be regulated by contract—death or personal injury from using a product—are extremely remote. ... But the greatest cost would not be the direct cost of drafting; it would be the cost of information. The inclusion of such a clause [dealing with potential liability] would not serve its intended purpose unless the consumer knew something about the costs of alternative safety measures that the producer might take and about the safety of competing products and brands. But the cost of generating that information and particularly the cost to the consumer of absorbing it, may well be disproportionate to the benefit of a negotiated (as distinct from imposed-by-law) level of safety.

What makes the problem of information serious is that the consumer may not have much intuitive feel for an extremely small risk. (pp. 280–81)

Landes and Posner also argue that a consumer would never voluntarily and with full knowledge agree to allow a manufacturer to be negligent (pp. 282).

Shavell agrees that if consumers correctly perceive risks, then contracts (in the form of warranties) between consumers and firms for allocating risks would be efficient, but that if consumers have erroneous perceptions, such warranties would not lead to efficient behavior for reasons similar to those advanced by Landes and Posner (pp. 61–62).

In a way, it is odd that the economic justification for replacing contract with tort in products liability rests on a deterrence theory. Priest (1985), in his essay on the origins of modern product liability law, demonstrates that supporters of such law (primarily Fleming James, with an assist from Friedrich Kessler's attack on contract) rested their case on a rationale of risk spreading (that is, compensation) and considered deterrence irrelevant. Epstein (1985) also indicates that insurance was a prime rationale of the expansion of product liability law. Thus, economists justify a legal doctrine with arguments explicitly rejected by those who were the leading advocates of adopting the law, and the economists reject the insurance function that advocates of the law used to justify its expansion. This position is not dispositive; the law could be serving a function that its founders did not understand or envision. There are several additional problems, however, with the economic analysis as typified by the Landes and Posner passage quoted above.

Inconsistencies

One problem is a lack of consistency between these arguments and arguments made elsewhere by Landes and Posner and by Shavell. Both treatises are generally based on complex economic analyses of tort law as providing incentives for efficient behavior in several contexts in addition to the producer-consumer context. They argue, for example, that, in torts involving strangers (those with no contractual relationship), legal standards such as negligence with a defense of contributory negligence are efficient, if the standard of care is chosen correctly. Similarly, pure negligence and comparative negligence are also efficient.[2] These legal standards will give both potential injurers and potential victims incentives to take optimal care.

But consider what is involved in enforcing a standard of negligence with a defense of contributory negligence. A victim is contributorily negligent, if he fails to take optimal precautions, given that the injurer was taking optimal precautions. A consumer (potential victim) must understand exactly what precautions a potential injurer should take and then understand exactly which precautions he (the victim) should take, given the optimal behavior of the injurer. Pedestrians and drivers, for example, must simultaneously decide how carefully to proceed, each assuming that the other has also made the correct decision.

I do not want to be interpreted as claiming that this analysis is incorrect or that the parties cannot undertake these seemingly complex calculations. It is standard economic analysis of response to incentives, and there is no reason to believe that injurers and victims cannot respond optimally to incentives, even if they cannot explicitly perform the required calculations. Economists generally assume ability of economic agents (consumers and producers) to respond to complex incentives, and I myself commonly make such assumptions (for example, Rubin 1983). What is inconsistent, however, is to argue that

---

[2]This result is standard in the economic analysis of law and goes back to Brown 1973, the first formal economic analysis of efficient tort law. Brown was incorrect on comparative negligence; for an analysis showing the efficiency of this standard, see Haddock and Curran 1985.

persons can optimally calculate the required behavior in stranger contexts but are unable to determine which contracts they should sign (or which warranties they should accept) in product liability contexts.

Accidents between strangers are approximately as rare as accidents involving products.[3] Therefore, it is not obvious that consumers would have better information about methods of preventing accidents in settings with strangers than about methods of preventing accidents in potential contractual settings. Landes-Posner and Shavell assume that consumers can make careful, complex calculations about risk in driving a car but are totally unable to make similar calculations in *buying* the car in the first place. Purchase of a product, however, is a one-time decision, and consumers may have the time and inclination to reflect on the costs and benefits involved. Conversely, many activities (such as driving) involve intense concentration, and a momentary slip can lead to a negligent accident. It is not at all obvious that the first decision is more difficult or less subject to rational calculation than is the latter decision.

It seems inconsistent to claim that problems of information would make contracts not feasible as a part of a more elaborate argument that relies on efficient response to incentives in situations where information is equally expensive and unavailable. That is, there is no reason to expect that tort law for interactions with strangers would provide efficient incentives for accident avoidance, if consumers are too ignorant to sign efficient accident avoidance contracts. Conversely, and of more relevance to my point, there is no reason to assume that consumers are able to make complex calculations regarding negligence standards but are unable to sign efficient risk spreading contracts.

Some Products Reduce Risk

A second problem with the Landes and Posner and the Shavell analyses is that both begin with the assumption that products add to injury risk.[4] Increasing the price of the product and reducing the level

---

[3]*National Safety Council* (1989) reports 1.8 motor vehicle-related disabling injuries, presumably between strangers, and 3.4 million home accidents, many presumably product-related (p. 2).

[4]This assumption dates to Spence 1977. It is the basis of Shavell's well-known paper on strict liability and negligence; Shavell 1980.

of consumption, as would occur if expected damages payments under tort raise the product's price, lead to reduced accidents. While this assumption appears natural, it is in many cases flawed. As discussed more fully in chapter 6, in many cases involving products liability the product actually reduces risk relative to nonuse of the product. This factor applies to medical care, pharmaceuticals, and many other goods and services involved in tort litigation. Airplanes, for example, are risk reducing relative to automobiles, which are themselves risk reducing relative to bicycles or motorcycles or horses. (For further discussion, see Huber 1985.)

For products that reduce risk, the general analysis of Landes and Posner and of Shavell, which assumes that products increase risk, is incorrect. For risk-increasing products, one purpose of tort law is to induce consumers to avoid overusing the product (what is called in the literature the activity level issue). For risk-reducing products, however, the goal of tort law should be to avoid discouraging use of products when the alternative is to accept even more risk. This goal requires focusing on the role of tort liability in affecting the price of the product. Contractual specification of damage payments will enable consumers to take account of price and compensation issues.

Limited Role of Contracts

My analysis so far would argue in favor of allowing contractual specification of liability rules in product injury cases, and indeed in all situations where consumers and producers are in contractual relations with each other. While I would generally favor such a solution, I do not need to go this far. In this book, I suggest contractual specification only of damage payments, not of liability rules. Even if we fully accept the arguments of Landes and Posner or of Shavell, this proposal is consistent with their reasoning, although they do not directly address the specific issue of contractual limits for damage amounts. The general arguments that they make against contractual specification of *liability rules*, however, do not apply to contractual specification of damage payments. Moreover, my argument says nothing about consumers accepting contracts allowing producers to be negligent, the second part of the Landes and Posner argument, since I do not deal with liability rules at all.

A key point made both by Landes and Posner and by Shavell is that with complex products consumers will not have adequate knowledge of accident avoidance technologies. According to Landes and Posner, "The growth in the technical complexity of products (the horse and buggy giving way to the automobile, patent medicines giving way to modern medicines, fresh foods giving way to canned and frozen foods, and so on) has been accompanied by a relative decline in the technical knowledge of consumers as consumers" (1987, p. 285). Shavell wrote, "In particular, customers' knowledge of risks attending the use of a wide class of modern-day products (automobiles, drugs, power machines) is presumably limited in significant ways because of consumers' quite natural inability to understand how the products function" (1987, p. 54).[5]

Even if we accept that this consumer ignorance means that consumers cannot efficiently specify by contract the appropriate level of care to be taken by manufacturers, this ignorance of technology has no implication for desired levels of compensation. That is, a consumer can measure the desired level of compensation for a mishap even if he knows nothing about the probability of the mishap or about the technology of accident causation or prevention. Moreover, in general, there is no relation between the cause of the accident and the desired form of compensation. A consumer might want to be reimbursed for medical expenses and lost earnings, but this desire is the same for any cause of injury or death. We all buy life and health insurance in which the payment does not, in general, depend on the cause of illness or death, and, in buying insurance, we need not consider the probabilities of each type of harm or the causes of various harms.

In addition, the form of desired compensation would be independent of the state of technology. A consumer may understand a horse better than a car but would want the same form of compensation if kicked by a horse or run over by a car. Therefore, arguments that changes in product liability law have been caused by the increasing complexity of products (Landes and Posner 1987, p. 284) do not

---

[5]The specific examples in the parentheses both of Landes and Posner and of Shavell are risk-reducing products. Modern medicines are safer and more effective than patent medicines; canned and frozen foods, by spreading the consumption of fruits and vegetables over the year and by reducing risks of contamination, are life enhancing; power machines, by reducing the amount of labor needed in heavy production tasks, are safety increasing. Even automobiles are safer per mile than horses and buggies.

explain changes in levels of damage awards.

Even if we accept the arguments of Landes and Posner and of Shavell regarding contractual specification of liability rules, these arguments say nothing about the desirability of contractual specification of damage amounts. In particular, if consumers would prefer *ex ante* not to pay for compensation for nonpecuniary damages, then they should be able to specify this in contracts, and their inability to understand injury mechanisms would be irrelevant.

Theoretical Difficulties

One point made by Landes and Posner is that their theory of the common law—that the law is efficient—is the only theory available. Indeed, the text of their book begins:

> This book explores the hypothesis that the common law is best explained as if the judges who created the law through decisions operating as precedents in later cases were trying to promote efficient resource allocation. We call this hypothesis the positive economic theory of tort law because no rival economic theory of tort law has been proposed. (1987, p. 1, emphasis in original)

There are two problems with this argument. First, Landes and Posner themselves find some parts of the law inefficient. They are then forced to rely on ad hoc appeals to various unmeasurable transactions costs to explain why some parts, but not others, are efficient. Second, there are other theories of the law that may be more general than the Landes and Posner theory in that they explain both those areas where the law appears to be efficient and areas where it appears inefficient (for example, Rubin 1982). These theories are also consistent with other economic theories of law.

Inefficient Laws. Landes and Posner claim that the common law of torts is inefficient in awarding damage payments in wrongful death cases. The law now awards pecuniary damages (payments to replace lost earnings) but not nonpecuniary damages (payments based, for example, on lost enjoyment of life). Landes and Posner admit that this is inconsistent with their theory, since they believe that the law should award such payments and is inefficient in not doing so.

I discuss this issue at length in chapter 4. There, I conclude that the law is actually efficient in not awarding such damage payments and that movements in the law to increase damage awards are inefficient. Thus, there is an argument that the common law was efficient in its awarding of damage amounts, and that in one area where Landes and Posner disagree with the law, they are incorrect.

Even if we believe their general theory, that the best positive theory of the common law is a search for economic efficiency, then my argument advanced here is at least as likely to be correct as their argument. They claim that the rules of third-party torts are efficient, and I have no quarrel with this claim; we agree on this point. They claim, however, that the rules of damage amounts in all wrongful death cases (normal torts and product liability torts) are incorrect in not allowing nonpecuniary damage payments; I claim that these rules are correct and efficient. I argue that the rules of product liability that deny consumers the right to contract are incorrect, and they claim that these rules are correct. Thus, it is not clear whether the Landes and Posner theory or the theory advanced here puts more faith in the efficiency of common law. We each find two of three doctrines efficient, and one inefficient.

An Alternative Theory. The alternative theory is that the law is shaped by litigants, rather than by judges.[6] Certain classes of litigants use the litigation process to seek certain outcomes. In this theory, the main pressure is from organized groups. That is, those types of litigants who can most easily organize use various tools (spending more on cases, relitigating until the law becomes favorable) to seek gains. This theory is a natural outgrowth of the now standard economic theory of legislation, as in Stigler 1988. It is also consistent with the Landes and Posner (1975) theory of judicial behavior with statutes, since they view statutes as the result of a bargain of an interest group with a legislature.

In this theory, the structure of the law can best be understood by examining the ability of different classes of litigants to organize and seek their goals. Tort law has been influenced by the ability of victims (or their attorneys) to organize. (This is discussed in Keenan and Rubin 1988. For a discussion of the Association of Trial Lawyers of America as an organized interest group with an interest in litigation from the

---

[6]This section is based on Rubin 1982, reprinted with modifications as chap. 2 of Rubin 1983. See also Rubin and Bailey 1992.

plaintiff's side, see Sowle 1991, pp. 37–41, and ATLA n.d.)

As transaction costs of organization change, the ability of various interest groups to become established also changes. Thus, possible victims of a class of accidents and their attorneys can now organize. Most major tort cases (Agent Orange, Bendectin, Johns-Manville and other asbestos cases, toxic shock, Dalkon shield, breast implants) show that there are organized groups of plaintiffs' attorneys. Organized public interest groups also participate in product liability litigation and receive financial support from plaintiff's attorneys. Marilyn Chase (1992) indicates that the Public Citizen Health Research Group (a Ralph Nader group, headed by Sidney Wolfe) has sold "how-to-sue" kits regarding breast implants, to plaintiffs' attorneys.

If plaintiffs' attorneys are a smaller, more easily organized group than defendants, then the theory discussed here argues that this could explain recent changes in tort law. If defendants can also organize, then they can work to change tort law. The theory does not distinguish between lobbying (using the legislature to achieve desired change) and litigation (seeking desirable precedents through the court system). Parties use whichever tool is most suitable for a given purpose.

This theory can explain both the relative efficiency of the law (common and statute) before about 1900, because costs of organization were too high, and the relative inefficiency of much law after that period, as various interest groups organized and used the law for rent-seeking purposes. It can also explain the current major battle between those in favor of maintaining or increasing the scope of current tort law and those in favor of returning to an earlier regime.[7] This battle is occurring on both the legislative and the litigation fronts, as the theory would indicate. Thus, the Landes and Posner theory may have been more appropriate in the nineteenth century, when the major body of common law evolved, than today.

Summary

The current standard economic theory of tort law (Shavell 1987; Landes and Posner 1987) suggests that contract would not be an

---

[7]This book is a part of that battle. It is possible, however, to evaluate intellectual arguments on their own merits, and I hope to convince the reader that the arguments are intellectually correct.

efficient solution to product liability law problems. This theory is flawed, however, in several dimensions. First, it assumes that consumers have the ability to perform all needed calculations in third-party accident situations (for example, in taking care when driving a car) but not in first-party situations (taking care in purchasing a car). There is no justification for such an assumption. Second, the theory assumes that products add to risk, but many products (and many involved in tort litigation) actually reduce risk. The Landes and Posner version of the theory assumes that tort law is efficient but also argues that some doctrines are inefficient. They also argue (incorrectly) that there is no alternative positive theory of law other than the efficiency theory. Therefore, the current theory cannot justify the arguments that contract is inefficient in tort law.

Even if this theory is correct, however, it applies to contractual negotiation over liability *rules*. The argument advanced in this book deals with *damage payments*, and the current theory says nothing about efficient contracting for payments. Thus, even if I am wrong and the current theory is correct, it is not inconsistent with my policy proposals.

4

Damage Payments
as Compensation

In considering tort damage payments as compensation for accidents involving purchased goods or services, the key point is that consumers would prefer payments for compensation much lower than those now awarded by the tort system. If consumers could contractually specify the level of damage awards from injuries involving product malfunctions, the best evidence indicates that they would not want to include some forms of compensation that the courts now award. In particular, consumers would want compensation only for lost earnings and for some part of medical expenses. They would not want compensation for pain and suffering, emotional distress, or hedonic values of life. They would not want the possibility of receiving large punitive damage payments. Virtually all economists who have studied the issue, including Landes-Posner and Shavell, agree that tort law is not an efficient mechanism for compensation.

In this chapter, after distinguishing between pecuniary and nonpecuniary losses and discussing their relationship to the marginal utility of wealth, I discuss the economics of insurance. This discussion is in two parts. This analysis indicates that consumers do not generally desire insurance against certain forms of harm and that the provision of such insurance through product liability doctrines will not benefit consumers. If consumers could freely contract, they would not want such damage awards to be paid after an accident.

One key point underlies the analysis. Before an accident occurs (a time called *ex ante* by economists), consumers would not want to pay the expected cost of certain forms of compensation to be paid after an accident. After an accident has occurred (*ex post*), if injured consumers have the right, then they will sue for whatever damage payments the courts will award. Thus, *ex ante,* consumers would be willing to sign contracts agreeing not to sue for certain forms of compensation. If the courts will not enforce these contracts, however, then injured consumers as plaintiffs *ex post* will attempt to gain these additional payments. The efficient level of damage payments is that which consumers want before they are injured, because, at this point, consumers compare the expected costs and benefits of alternative levels of payments. It is for this reason that enforceable contracts are necessary.

Some Definitions

Pecuniary and Nonpecuniary Losses. Economists commonly distinguish between two types of harms or losses that may occur as a result of an accident. *Pecuniary* losses are those which can be fully replaced by some payment of money. These would include lost earnings, costs of medical care, and losses of property (a damaged car, a house destroyed by fire). Consumers commonly insure against pecuniary losses. Some examples are medical insurance against the out-of-pocket costs of illness or injury; insurance for lost earnings; property insurance on large, high-valued items such as cars and houses; and life insurance to replace the family's share of lost earnings of the family breadwinner if he should die.

Nonpecuniary losses cannot be replaced. Pain and suffering is a nonpecuniary loss. So are losses associated with many forms of injury, such as a lost limb. (If this lowers potential earnings or increases costs of specially modified automobiles, for example, then these costs would be pecuniary, as would medical costs.) A relatively new form of damage payments awarded by some courts, lost enjoyment of life (sometimes called hedonic damages) is also a nonpecuniary loss. In some cases, courts have awarded damage payments for worry associated with a potential loss, such as the fear that a heart valve may break. This is a nonpecuniary loss. Loss of some forms of property, such as family pictures or heirlooms, with little monetary but large sentimental value, or even the family dog, would entail nonpecuniary loss. The ultimate nonpecuniary loss is death of oneself or of one's relatives. Consumers never voluntarily insure against nonpecuniary losses.

Pecuniary and nonpecuniary losses differ in their effects on the consumers' utility function, as discussed next. Analysis of the effect of these losses on the utility function shows why it is rational for consumers to forgo insurance against nonpecuniary losses and why provision of such insurance through the tort system is inefficient.

Marginal Utility of Wealth. The *utility function* represents the relation between happiness and wealth. Everyone is happier with more wealth. That is, for everyone total utility increases as wealth increases, or, mathematically, the utility function has a positive slope. What is of interest for many problems, however, is the rate at which happiness increases as wealth increases. This rate of change is what is called the *marginal utility of wealth.*

In theory, happiness (utility) can increase at the same rate as income, at a lower rate, or at a higher rate. If utility and wealth increase at the same rate, there is said to be constant marginal utility of wealth. If utility increases faster than wealth, there is said to be increasing marginal utility of wealth.

In general, evidence indicates, for most consumers, a decreasing marginal utility of wealth: the marginal utility of wealth decreases as levels of wealth increase. Figure 4–1 shows the relation between total utility and wealth; the slope of the total utility curve is the marginal utility of wealth. Since the curve becomes flatter (the slope decreases) as wealth increases, the marginal utility of wealth is decreasing with increases in wealth.[1] (The curve is everywhere positively sloped, indicating increasing total utility as wealth increases.)

This decreasing marginal utility explains why consumers are risk averse. Most consumers will not accept an exactly fair gamble for large sums of money. Most of us would not bet half of our annual salary on the toss of a coin: the increase in utility from gaining an extra half year's salary is less than the loss in utility from losing the same amount of money. As we will see, risk aversion also explains the purchase of insurance for some potential large losses, such as a house fire.

This concept is relevant to the analysis of optimal compensation for accidental losses, because different types of losses have different effects on the marginal utility of wealth. Pecuniary losses reduce the

---

[1]Constant utility would be shown by a straight line, and increasing marginal utility, by a curve that became steeper as we moved to the right. In what follows, however, I consider only decreasing marginal utility, since this is the most empirically relevant case.

FIGURE 4–1
DECREASING MARGINAL UTILITY OF WEALTH

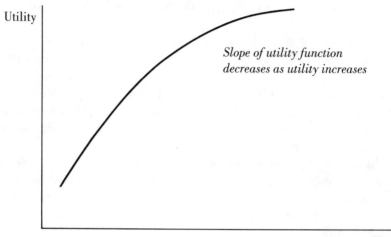

Slope of utility function
decreases as utility increases

SOURCE: Author.

total utility of wealth but leave the schedule relating wealth and utility unchanged. In figure 4–2, a pecuniary loss is a movement from *A* to *B*. The total amount of wealth is reduced, but the schedule is unchanged. As the total amount of wealth is reduced, the marginal utility increases because of the assumption of diminishing marginal utility. (Marginal utility diminishes with increases in wealth, so it increases with reductions in wealth, such as from an accidental pecuniary loss.) If our house burns down (neglecting insurance), we move from *A* to *B*; we are poorer, and therefore our marginal utility of wealth is higher. We want money to buy a new house to replace the loss. As we see below, consumers would want to insure against this sort of loss. (The analysis is from Cook and Graham 1977; Rea 1982; and Graham and Pierce 1984.)

Nonpecuniary losses do not merely move consumers along a fixed utility function. They actually change the utility function. That is, as a result of a nonpecuniary loss, the relation between income and wealth is altered. There are several possible changes.

One possibility is that the nonpecuniary loss merely shifts the utility function downward in a parallel move without any effect on marginal utility; this is shown in figure 4–3. In this case, the consumer

32

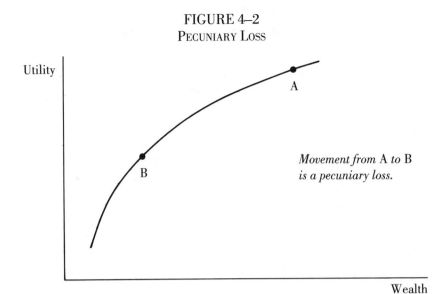

FIGURE 4–2
PECUNIARY LOSS

Utility

A

Movement from A to B
is a pecuniary loss.

B

Wealth

SOURCE: Author.

is worse off as a result of the accident because total utility is reduced, but the marginal utility of wealth is unchanged at any income level. That is, the slope of the total utility curve is unchanged at any level of income. A loss such as the loss of the family heirloom would represent this type of shift. An important point, developed more fully in the next section, is that consumers would not want to insure against this sort of nonpecuniary loss.

An even more severe case is that in which the accident changes the slope as well as the level of the marginal utility schedule, as shown in figure 4–4. Here, for any given level of wealth, the consumer derives less utility from an additional dollar after the accident than before. One example is a serious injury that reduces the ability of the consumer to enjoy consumption.[2] An even more extreme example is death: with death, the marginal utility of wealth is zero for the decedent.

---

[2]In theory, such an accident might increase the marginal utility of wealth. Empirical evidence (Viscusi and Evans 1990) indicates, however, that this is not typically what happens. Rather, accidents typically reduce the marginal utility of wealth, presumably by reducing the ability of injured consumers to enjoy consumption activities.

FIGURE 4–3
NONPECUNIARY LOSS WITH NO CHANGE IN MARGINAL UTILITY

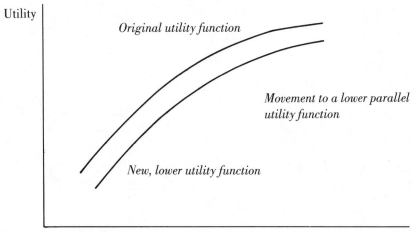

SOURCE: Author.

For a tragic but informative example, consider the effect on the utility of parents' wealth of the death of a child. Clearly, total utility (general happiness) is greatly reduced: there is probably no more tragic event. Marginal utility of wealth is also reduced. That is, the value of additional money is reduced. Parents will not need money to feed, clothe, and educate the deceased child. Thus, a policy that provides parents with additional wealth in the event of such a death will not necessarily be worth its cost. This is consistent with the observation that parents seldom insure the lives of their children.

Purpose of Insurance

Consider a possible accident that reduces the level of wealth but does not change the utility schedule; that is, consider an accident leading to a pecuniary loss. A paradigmatic example is the loss of a house to a fire without personal injury or death (and, for simplicity, no irreplaceable heirlooms or pets are lost in the fire).

Consider now two possible states of the world: one in which the accident occurs and one in which the accident does not occur. (The

FIGURE 4–4
NONPECUNIARY LOSS WITH REDUCTION IN MARGINAL UTILITY

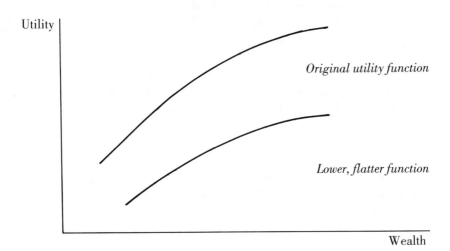

SOURCE: Author.

state in which the accident does not occur is much more probable than the state in which it does occur.) If the consumer does not have insurance, then marginal utility of wealth is much higher (because wealth is much lower) in the state with the accident. (This would be equivalent to a move from *A* to *B* in figure 4–2.) As a result, the consumer would like to transfer wealth from the no-accident state to the accident state because he would gain utility by such a transfer. Since the marginal utility is lower in the no-accident state, the loss in utility from reducing wealth by one dollar in the no-accident state would be less than the gain in utility from increasing wealth by one dollar in the accident state. (This depends on the assumption of risk aversion.) The consumer would like to continue this process until the marginal utility of wealth is exactly the same in both states of the world. At this point total utility is maximized.[3]

---

[3]Those familiar with economics will recognize this as a simple maximization problem, of the sort commonly encountered in economic analysis. The structure of the problem is to maximize expected utility (utility weighted by probabilities) across various states of the world, subject to a total wealth constraint. The equalization of marginal utilities is the first-order condition for solving this maximization problem.

Insurance allows the consumer to transfer wealth from low marginal utility states of the world to high marginal utility states and thus to maximize expected utility. Consider the example of the house fire. Let there be a 1 percent chance of a house fire in any year that will destroy a $100,000 house. The actuarially fair price of insurance is $1,000 per year. If the consumer purchases insurance, he is $1,000 poorer in the state of the world in which the house does not burn down and $100,000 richer in the state in which it does burn down.[4] The consumer has effectively transferred wealth across states of the world in exactly the manner discussed: he has reduced wealth in the low-marginal-utility state (the no-accident state, where wealth is reduced by the $1,000 premium) and increased it in the high-marginal-utility state of the world (the fire state, where actual wealth is increased by the $100,000 payment from the insurance company). This has maximized the expected utility.

Synthesis

We are now ready to put the pieces together. Pecuniary losses shift the consumer downward along a utility function and thus increase the marginal utility of wealth. It is therefore desirable to insure against pecuniary losses (when the cost of insurance is not too high), and most consumers do insure against such losses. We all carry fire insurance. Many of us have life insurance to replace earnings lost by our families if we die. We also insure against many other large pecuniary losses.

Nonpecuniary losses, conversely, do not increase the marginal utility of wealth. Some losses leave it unchanged, but many of those involved in product liability cases reduce the marginal utility of wealth. We would not expect consumers to insure against such losses, and, indeed, we observe that they do not. Some examples follow.

Death of a Breadwinner. Consider a family with one earner. The family depends on this person for its income. If the breadwinner dies,

---

[4] Actually, the consumer would have to pay more than $1,000 for the insurance, because of the costs of selling and administering the insurance. With a premium not too much greater than $1,000, the consumer would still benefit from the insurance; the amount above $1,000 that a given consumer would be willing to pay would depend on his degree of risk aversion. As we see below, consumers are not infinitely risk averse, so a high enough premium would discourage purchase of insurance.

then the family will be poorer (without insurance), and therefore the marginal utility of wealth will be higher. We would therefore expect families to insure against this loss, and, indeed, most breadwinners with children carry insurance for their families in the event of death of the main earner. This death creates a pecuniary loss to the survivors. The amount of insurance that should be carried should be the earnings over and above the amount that the breadwinner would have consumed, since this is the loss to the survivors. If the breadwinner dies, the family will suffer a nonpecuniary loss as well (assuming normal patterns of love and affection), but we would not expect and do not observe insurance against this loss.

Death of a Child. To see this last point more clearly, consider the example of the death of a child. Most families do not carry life insurance on their children. (Some carry enough to bury a child, a pecuniary loss.) This is not because the families do not love the child or because they will not suffer a loss in the death. It is because, while there is a major loss, the loss does not increase the marginal utility of wealth but rather reduces it.

What would be involved if the family did purchase life insurance on a young child? Assume that a $100,000 life insurance policy could be purchased for $50 per year, approximately the actuarial price. Then, if the child lives, the family, which has expenses associated with feeding and clothing the child, is $50 poorer. If the child dies, then the family has less need for money but is $100,000 richer. This is not a good trade for the family, and it is not surprising that virtually no one carries life insurance on a child.

Serious Injury. Assume that a person suffers serious injury and that the injury will never be cured. One is paralyzed, for example, and confined to a wheelchair, or loses a limb.

This creates increased value for medical care—the marginal utility of wealth used to purchase medical care increases. As a result, we would expect, and we observe, people purchasing insurance for medical care in the event of injury. Conversely, the marginal utility of additional wealth is reduced to a level below its value in the uninjured state. Therefore, we would not expect people to replace fully income for disability, and we do not observe such full replacement.

The injury also creates a large nonpecuniary loss, since utility is much lower as a result of such an accident. Nonetheless, we would not expect people to insure against this loss, and, indeed, they do not.

Slight Injury. Finally, consider a minor injury that will entail some medical expenses, some loss of work, and some pain, but from which there will be full recovery. We would expect, and we observe, consumers insuring against the first two components of loss. Medical insurance covers medical costs of injuries. Most jobs involve compensation for days off due to sickness or injury. Firms offer such compensation because workers implicitly demand it and it provides efficient insurance. Conversely, there is virtually no market for insurance for pain and suffering. Apparently consumers do not find such insurance worth buying. This is again consistent with the theory: pain and suffering does not raise the marginal utility of wealth and so does not create a demand for insurance.

In Sum. Consumers buy insurance to equate marginal utilities in possible states of the world. Pecuniary losses such as loss of income from an injury, loss of earnings from a breadwinner, or loss of a house from a fire increase the marginal utility of wealth, and consumers shift income to such accident states by purchasing insurance. Some harms (severe incurable injury, pain and suffering, death) do not lead to increased marginal utility of wealth, and consumers do not insure against these harms.

Croley and Hanson (1990, n. 200) claim that consumers do sometimes buy insurance against nonpecuniary losses. As examples, they suggest dismemberment insurance, life insurance on children, and insurance clauses that double payments for accidental death (double indemnity). Priest (1992, pp. 246–48) addresses these issues and indicates that none of these are necessarily for nonpecuniary losses. He indicates that Croley and Hanson provide no rationale for believing that dismemberment insurance is for nonpecuniary losses. Life insurance on children is mostly for small amounts, approximating the cost of burial. The rest is mostly whole life insurance, which incorporates a large savings component. Double-indemnity life insurance is puzzling, but Priest suggests that those dying accidently are less likely to have their financial affairs in order than are those dying from other causes. It is fair to say that there is no evidence of widespread or substantial purchase of insurance against nonpecuniary losses, which is consistent with the theory. Even if *some* consumers do *sometimes* purchase such insurance, there is no reason to make it mandatory for *all* consumers in buying *all* products.

Implications

These results have important implications for damage payments for an injury as a result of a tort. In particular, since consumers do not want compensation for nonpecuniary losses, then *ex ante* (before the accident occurs) consumers would prefer not to pay the expected cost of compensation to be awarded for this class of harms if an accident should occur. That is, consumers would prefer that the price of a product be lower and not include insurance for nonpecuniary losses.

After an accident occurs, an injured consumer (or the estate of a dead consumer) will seek compensation for nonpecuniary losses if allowed to do so. Producers, knowing that consumers will behave this way, will charge a price for the product that includes the expected compensation for nonpecuniary damage awards, unless they believe that the courts will enforce contractual limits on such payments.

This is the first major substantive point of the analysis. If they could do so, consumers would prefer to sign binding contracts limiting their ability to seek compensation for nonpecuniary losses from an accident.

Even for pecuniary losses, there is an issue. Many injured persons already have insurance themselves. Persons will have insurance coverage, for example, for lost wages through sick pay or through disability insurance. For these people, tort damage awards will serve as an extra payment. As argued above, however, injured persons desire less, not more, income, and so the prospect of additional income in an injured state will not be worth its cost. (The same point applies to medical care, discussed more fully in the next section.)

A method of handling this problem is for payments from the injurer to be paid to the injured's insurance company, if the injured is insured. (In insurance terminology, this is called subrogation.) Such payments would not directly affect the price that consumers would pay for the product, since the payments from the producer would not be, in general, any lower. (As indicated below, this is not true for medical payments.) If product liability payments generally went to direct insurers, however, then costs of direct insurance would be reduced.

Thus, consumers might want their own insurance policies to be written with clauses that would require subrogation. If so, the courts should enforce these clauses.

(The alternative would be to reduce product liability payments if the injured already had insurance, called collateral sources. The collateral source rule says that consumers can collect both from their first-party insurance and from the product causing the injury. Increasing subrogation is more efficient than modification of the collateral source rule. Modification of the rule might provide insufficient incentives for producers to take care. The incentive problem is addressed more fully in chapter 5.)

Adverse Selection and Moral Hazard

In addition to not wanting damage payments for pain and suffering, there are other contractual limits on awards that consumers would seek *ex ante* if they could do so.[5] These arise from other aspects of the problems of compensation as insurance. There are two problems that limit the ability of markets to offer insurance and that can make insurance contracts inefficient where they do exist. These are adverse selection, which occurs before insurance is purchased, and moral hazard, which occurs after insurance is purchased. Both of these affect compensation desired *ex ante* by consumers from a product-related injury.

Adverse Selection. This occurs when a potential insured has relevant information about his own risk that is lacking to the insurance company. If clients can predict better than the insurance company that they are at risk of some mishap, then there are problems with insurance markets. In the limit, this problem can cause the market to cease.

Rather than an analytical explanation, an example may clarify what is involved. Some years ago, the Washington, D.C., city council passed a law forbidding insurance companies from testing potential clients for HIV, the precursor to AIDS. Insurance providers im-

---

[5]The analysis of moral hazard and of adverse selection is common in economics; for a discussion, see Rubin 1990. The application to problems of products liability and tort law is from an important paper by Priest (1987), although the specific recommendations should not necessarily be attributed to him.

mediately ceased offering new life insurance policies to residents of the District and did not again sell such insurance until Congress forced repeal of the law. That is, immediately on passage of the law, the market for life insurance in the District ceased. This cessation was the result of an extreme problem of adverse selection.

Why? Consumers themselves could have HIV tests performed and determine if they had the disease. Thus, before purchasing insurance, a consumer could know if he was likely to get AIDS, but the insurance company could not have access to the same information. Then it would have paid for anyone who tested positive to purchase large amounts of insurance. The price of insurance reflected the risk of dying for the general population, but those who tested positive had a much greater chance of dying (faced a much larger risk), and therefore life insurance would have been a good buy for such persons.

Insurance companies could not determine who tested positive, because of the law. Therefore, had they continued to offer insurance, they would have provided insurance at normal rates to those at extremely high risk of death. This would have led to large losses by the insurance companies. To avoid the ensuing bankruptcy, insurance companies ceased operating. The pool of insureds would have contained a much greater percentage of persons with HIV-positive tests than would the general population, and so the cost to the insurance companies would have been much greater than from a randomly selected group of persons. The risk pool for the insurance company would have been too wide, including both HIV-positive and normal persons.

This is an extreme example of adverse selection, but it does illustrate the relevant point. Adverse selection can hinder and, in the limit, eliminate insurance markets. It is always in the interest of insurance companies to narrow risk pools as much as possible. That is, it is in their interest to determine as precisely as possible the relative risk of each potential client. If clients know something about themselves that insurance companies do not know, then there will be a general tendency for the lowest risk consumers to refrain from purchase of insurance and for high-risk consumers to purchase the insurance.

Consumers lose from risk pools that are too broad. (In the D.C. example, the risk pool was overly broad because it would have included both HIV persons and those who did not test positive for

HIV.) In the extreme case, they lose because the market will cease. Even in less extreme situations, however, some consumers lose because either they are paying too much for insurance or because they choose not to purchase any insurance at all. (Even though consumers are generally risk averse, they are not infinitely risk averse. As the cost to consumers of insurance increases above the mathematically fair level, some consumers will drop out of the market.)

The relevance of this point becomes clear when we realize that damage payments at tort viewed as a compensation device have many of the characteristics of insurance. It is insurance that is bundled with the product. Moreover, if the courts will not honor contracts limiting damage payments, then it is insurance that the consumer must buy and pay for if he buys the product, whether he wants the insurance or not.

Adverse selection is a problem with all insurance contracts. When insurance is explicitly offered as insurance, however, sellers are able to devise mechanisms that limit adverse selection by narrowing risk pools. Teenage drivers, drivers with bad accident records, and drivers of "hot" cars, for example, pay higher automobile accident premiums than middle-aged safe drivers of Volvos. Owners of brick homes near hydrants pay less for fire insurance than owners of wood homes in isolated areas. Overweight smokers pay more for life insurance than others, and men pay more than women, since men die younger. (For the same reason, women pay more for retirement insurance.) Indeed, insurance companies compete partly by finding criteria that narrow risk classes because this gives the companies a competitive advantage for the low-risk consumers with respect to that criteria. When insurance is sold bundled with products, anyone buying the product also buys the insurance, and the ability to control adverse selection is greatly reduced.

One component in which clients can differ is the amount of insurance. Consider life insurance. A policy for $1 million is a higher risk policy to an insurance company than is a policy for $100,000 for a consumer with otherwise identical characteristics, such as age and health status. That is, if the former insured dies, then the payment is greater than if the latter dies. Insurance companies obviously separate the risks associated with the $1 million policy from those associated with the $100,000 policy by charging a different fee for each. They do not average the two charges and charge the same premium for both policies. If they did, there would be adverse selection in that the $1 million policyholder would gladly buy the insurance, but the $100,000 policyholder would not. The notion of charging the same amount for policies with different values strikes us as absurd.

Although this notion is absurd, it is the standard way in which insurance through the tort system operates. Some airplane passengers earn $500,000 per year, and their estates may collect $5 million if they die in a crash; others earn and will collect one-tenth as much. Nonetheless, if they fly in the same class, they pay the same amount for their tickets. But the tickets have the insurance bundled with them, and part of the price goes to pay for the insurance. Therefore, the tort system is forcing consumers into exactly the position that was seen to be absurd in the context of the purchase of direct life insurance. Two persons are purchasing wildly different amounts of insurance but paying the same price.

This policy also acts generally as a wealth transfer from the poor, who stand to collect relatively small payments because of death or injury, to the rich, who stand to collect more. Thus, in addition to being inefficient, this policy violates our notions of fairness.

If consumers could choose, they would not choose to be aggregated into one risk pool for insurance. Rather, low-risk consumers would prefer to be in pools with other low-risk consumers, and high-risk consumers would not be able to achieve a subsidy from the low-risk consumers. Since in the issues at hand risk is often associated with income, elimination of the forced transfer from the tort system would conform with general notions of fairness as well as being efficient.

Adverse selection operates in other ways within the tort system. Different models of a similar product, for example, may be aimed at different classes of users. These different models may have different safety features. A chain saw produced for professional lumberjacks may have fewer safety features than a model produced for consumer use in cutting firewood. If the consumer buys the professional model and is injured, he may now have a tort action. In the past, the doctrine of assumption of risk might have made such a suit impossible, but the courts now limit the applicability of this doctrine. A consumer desiring to purchase the professional model might be willing to waive his right to damage compensation if he could do so.

This is the second major substantive point of the analysis. If they could do so, consumers might prefer to sign binding contracts limiting the total amount of compensation for even pecuniary losses from an accident.

Moral Hazard. This is a situation in which behavior is affected by the existence of insurance. Someone may not lock his car, for example, because he knows that if it is stolen the insurance company will compensate him for the loss. Insurance contracts are written to reduce moral hazard.

With product liability, moral hazard arises primarily after an injury. That hazard may occur with medical costs. Medical costs are an important component of tort liability. Direct (first-party) medical insurance uses several mechanisms to reduce moral hazard, and it is important to examine these mechanisms within the context of product liability.

It may seem that an injured person with a given injury needs a certain amount of medical care and that the amount is not under the control of the patient. This is incorrect. There are many ways in which consumers with similar injuries can use different amounts of medical care. The amount used depends on the cost to the consumer himself. Consumers who must pay 20 percent of the cost of hospitalization, for example, may be more likely to use a semiprivate room than a private room. It is also possible to use more or less full-time nursing care for a given injury.

Two mechanisms that serve to reduce this problem with first-party insurance are *coinsurance* and *deductibles*. With coinsurance, the insured pays part of the costs of any medical care. That is, the insurance company may pay 80 percent of medical costs, but the insured pays the rest. Such coinsurance gives patients some incentive to economize on medical care.

A deductible is a payment that the insured must make before coverage begins. A medical insurance policy may require that the insured pay the first $200 per year of medical bills before the insurance begins to cover remaining costs. Again, this is a method of providing an incentive for the insured to economize on medical care.

Medical insurers also specify in some detail the amount that they will pay for any particular condition. This limits spending. An extreme version is a health maintenance organization, a situation in which the consumer in a healthy state contracts for medical care from a provider who will pay costs but will also determine treatment. Again, this is a method of limiting the moral hazard associated with medical insurance.

The consumer decides *ex ante* (before he is sick or injured) exactly what sort of medical care he will receive if he becomes sick or injured. *Ex post*, the consumer would want the maximum amount of medical care because the consumer knows that he is injured and will benefit from care. The correct measure of value, however, is the *ex ante* willingness to pay for insurance, at a time when the consumer is comparing expected costs and benefits and before he knows if he will be a beneficiary or not.

If tort damage payments allow full compensation for all medical care expenses, then the consumer will use the maximum possible. The proper amount (the amount that the consumer would be willing to pay for in the price of the product), however, would correspond to the consumer's freely chosen level of medical insurance. Thus, for those consumers who have medical insurance, the proper solution is for their normal medical insurance (with all its limits and constraints, including any coinsurance or deductible) to govern and for the injurer to reimburse the medical insurance company for its expenses. This would also imply subrogation (compensation of the injured's own insurance company for any costs), so that the injured could not collect twice for the same injury. Cooter and Sugarman (1988) also argue that the injured party's own health insurance is relevant in deciding on the level of compensation for an injury.

In today's society, consumers actually carry more insurance than would be optimal. The tax system creates a large subsidy to insurance, since dollars spent by employers on health insurance are not taxed as income. As a result, medical expenses paid through insurance are paid with before-tax dollars. Therefore, policies have lower deductibles and less coinsurance than consumers would choose if they were using real, after-tax dollars. Thus, arguing for replacement of tort damage payments with the level of insurance that consumers actually carry is still biasing the result toward excessive payment but payments preferable to those involved in tort.

For consumers without insurance, some standard such as the level that Medicare or a large private insurer would pay for a comparable injury would be appropriate. Indeed, defendants might prefer to hire some large private insurance company to monitor the payments to an injured plaintiff.

This is the third major substantive point of the analysis. If they could do so, consumers would prefer to sign binding contracts limiting their medical compensation to the amount covered by their private insurance or, for uninsured consumers, to the amount that a large private insurer would pay for the injury.

A Note on Punitive Damages

Punitive damage payments are payments above and beyond the amount desired for compensation, however that is computed. Thus, to the extent that this form of damage awards provides even more payment than that provided for compensation (which is itself more than consumers would want), then consumers *ex ante* would not want to be able to sue for such payments. The purpose of punitive damage payments is not compensation but rather deterrence. (I discuss this form of payments in chapter 5.) The fourth point is that, if they were able to do so, consumers would prefer to limit their ability to sue for punitive damage payments to truly outrageous cases, perhaps those where outright fraud was committed by the manufacturer.

Damage Payments as Lotteries?

It may appear that consumers value the chance of large damage payments as a form of lottery. After all, we do observe many consumers buying lottery tickets even though these have negative expected values (since the seller makes a profit on the ticket). The tort system, however, is not an efficient method of buying a lottery ticket, even if it is desired. There are two reasons for this inefficiency.

First, if we consider the legal fees involved, including both the contingent fee going to the plaintiff's lawyer and the cost of the defendant's lawyer, which is also factored into the product price, then these may approximate two-thirds of the total award. That is, for every dollar consumers pay for tort insurance bundled with products, they get back about 33 cents. This is a much worse return than from a real lottery.

Second, the tort system is a peculiar lottery: it pays off only if the consumer is severely injured or killed. As stressed throughout the chapter, injured consumers place a lower value on wealth than do healthy consumers. Therefore, the tort system pays off only under those conditions where the money is worth relatively little, another undesirable feature of the tort system as a lottery. For both these reasons, consumers who want to gamble would be better off buying the product unbundled from the tort liability and using the savings to purchase lottery tickets.

Summary

As of now, consumers cannot sign binding contracts to limit damage payments for an injury associated with a product or service, even though the consumer is in an *ex ante* contractual relationship with the injurer. Therefore, we cannot directly observe the contracts that the consumer would sign. Theoretical analysis indicates, however, that these contracts would have several identifiable features:

1.   The contracts would call for no compensation for nonpecuniary losses (losses of items that cannot be replaced). Thus, there would be no compensation for pain and suffering or for worry about potential risks. Compensation for death would be limited to the economic loss to survivors. Compensation for serious irreparable injury would be limited to medical expenses, as defined below, and lost earnings.

2.   Even for pecuniary losses, the contracts would call for an upper bound, which might approximate the expected pecuniary loss for the lowest risk consumer of the product. This would at least partially control adverse selection in product purchases.

3.   For medical payments, the coverage would be equal to coverage that the consumer himself had purchased from his own medical insurance company. For an uninsured consumer, coverage would be equal to what would be provided by an agency such as Medicare or by a large private insurance company. This action would reduce or eliminate moral hazard in the use of medical care.

4.   Consumers would greatly limit their ability to seek punitive damages.

In addition, consumers might choose to contract with their own disability and health insurance. In both cases, they might want to contract for subrogation, compensation to their own insurance companies by the injurer. In an injured state, money does not have increased marginal utility, and so consumers would not want to be paid twice for

47

lost time and for medical expenses.[6]

Most of the reasoning in this chapter is based on theoretical analysis, not on empirical observation, since we do not see such contracts written. As indicated in chapter 1, however, there is little cost if the analysis is wrong. If we allow free contract and if I am mistaken, then consumers will not choose the terms that I have predicted.

Conversely, if we allow free contract and consumers do choose such terms, then we should realize that this choice is due to rational behavior and is not a choice imposed by firms. Arguments based on the undesirability of contracts of adhesion, unconscionability, or unequal bargaining power are not needed to explain consumers' choices if they choose in ways consistent with the above analysis. Thus, the arguments in this chapter can provide a defense, if consumers sign such contracts and later attempt to obtain payments for some of the damages excluded by contract.

---

[6]Priest (1992) indicates that subrogation is already common in both workmen's compensation and first-party health insurance (p. 258).

5

Damage Payments
as Deterrence

In addition to compensating those harmed, damage payments serve a deterrence function. The goal of deterrence is to force decision makers to bear the costs of their actions. In this way, if a manufacturer does not take efficient precautions, he must pay the costs of the injury. If the manufacturer is liable for these costs, it is in his interest to take efficient precautions and to avoid paying damages. Efficient precautions are those whose value to the potential victim is at least as great as their cost. Potential victims would be willing to pay a price for products that included the cost of efficient precautions, and it is desirable to penalize manufacturers who do not take this level of precautions.

Because first-party insurance is generally available to compensate the injured, most economists believe that the major function of tort law and damage payments is deterrence. (This includes Landes-Posner and Shavell, some of the strongest defenders within the economics profession of modern tort law.) In this view, the main reason that damages are paid to the party actually injured (instead of, for example, to the state) is to provide an incentive for the harmed individual to bring suit. (Payment of damages to the victim also provides a benefit by reducing the incentives of potential victims to take excessive precautions to avoid accidents.)

The deterrence justification for damages payments is to prevent situations in which consumers would have preferred to pay the cost of actions to reduce risk, but the actions were not taken. Payments for hedonic damage (discussed in chapter 6), the measure of lost enjoyment of life, which is based on a linear extrapolation from willingness to pay for a marginal reduction in risk, is the penalty needed to induce optimal precautions if the potential injurer would otherwise take no precautions at all (Spence 1977; Shavell 1987, chap. 10). If the manufacturer faces other incentives to take precautions, however, the willingness-to-pay measure of damages is too large.

If consumers have perfect information about product risks, then there is no need for the tort system as deterrence at all. This is the mirror image of the situation in which only the tort system provides deterrence and full damage payments are optimal. While theoretical economic analysis is easier if an extreme assumption (only torts deter, or there is complete information and so no need of torts) is made, in the real world neither extreme theoretical assumption is correct. Rather, consumers have some incomplete and sometimes erroneous information about risks, and torts are one imperfect instrument, among many, for deterrence. Indeed, one function of the tort system may be viewed as providing consumers direct information, as when consumers learn from news reports about product litigation. This information is imperfect, but it does exist and does provide incentives for safety. For practical policy (as opposed to theoretical analysis), we cannot ignore this information and argue that only tort damage payments provide deterrence.

Because the market almost always provides significant precautionary incentives, often at the optimal level and sometimes beyond, it is incorrect to view the willingness-to-pay measure as the only source of deterrence. Damage payments are seldom if ever the only instrument used for deterrence. Indeed, the most widely used measures of willingness to pay for safety are values derived from wage differentials for risky jobs. These differentials would not exist were it not for market-based precautionary incentives, which imply that workers have good information about risk. Damage payments cannot be the only source of deterrence.

Direct Safety Regulation

One impetus for safety in addition to tort law is direct safety regulation. Such regulation applies to many of the products at issue in litigation. Pharmaceuticals must be approved by the Food and Drug Administration before sale. Evidence indicates that this agency is too restrictive, rather than too lenient, in approving drugs (Peltzman 1973; Comanor

1986). Therefore, it is highly unlikely that any approved drug (without outright fraud in the approval process) is unsafe and unlikely that tort liability associated with pharmaceuticals will lead to efficient increases in safety.

The Occupational Safety and Health Administration regulates workplace safety. The Consumer Product Safety Commission regulates many consumer products; the FDA and the Department of Agriculture regulate the quality of foods. The National Highway and Traffic Safety Administration regulates automobiles. The Environmental Protection Agency regulates environmental risks. Physicians cannot practice medicine unless they are licensed.

I am not claiming that the existence of these agencies is always enough so that tort law cannot ever lead to efficient improvements in safety, nor do I claim that this regulation is optimal. My point is much more modest. Since these forces additional to tort law do exist, it is clearly improper to design deterrence mechanisms as if tort law were the only force for safety. There is no reason to assume that an additional incentive must always be constructed through large liability payments. In most situations, this additional incentive leads to precautions greater than consumers wish to pay for. Even when a firm does underinvest in safety, deterrence mechanisms other than the liability system come into action to penalize firms that spend too little on safety. Because this is an essential point, I discuss it in some detail, first in the context of workplace and then product safety.

Workplace Safety

There is no reason to expect that, in any systematic sense, too little is spent on safety in the workplace. Indeed, the data used to calculate the willingness to pay (hedonic) values are based on an explicit assumption that wages vary with job risk. Most values are obtained from labor market analyses of wage differentials and job risks. Analysts observe small differences in pay for jobs with small levels of associated risk.[1] A job with a .0001 risk of death per year, for example, may pay a wage premium of $300. This would lead to a hedonic value of $3 million.

This method of derivation, however, indicates that in general workers are paid *ex ante* (before any injury) to bear on-the-job risks. It

---

[1]In the modern American economy, no jobs are associated with large risks of death.

is therefore incorrect to use the values for compensation for job-related deaths. If workers are reasonably rational and aware of risks (as they must be to generate the wage differentials in the first place), then they are compensated for bearing these risks through the wage payment for the job. This compensation, with no help from the liability system, provides an exactly correct incentive for employers to spend optimally on safety. If the willingness-to-pay figures have any meaning, they imply that in labor market situations there is no gain from paying *ex post* (after the accident) compensation in addition to the *ex ante* payment for risk bearing. If workers are not compensated for risk bearing through *ex ante* wage payments, the calculated hedonic values themselves are meaningless. In this case, there is no theoretical basis for using such values for *ex post* compensation.[2]

Therefore, compensation as hedonic damage payments after injury would amount to compensating workers twice for the same risk: once *ex ante* through higher wage payments and once *ex post* through damage payments. The effect of this double compensation would be harmful to workers. Faced with the prospect of double compensation— which in many respects acts as a tax on employment—employers would take too many precautions (from the viewpoint of workers) and hire too few workers.

It might appear that employers could reduce the wage paid to workers by the cost of the expected damage payment for death. This is where the insurance issue, discussed in chapter 4, becomes relevant. A large payment to heirs for death, in addition to insurance voluntarily purchased by workers, is not worth its *ex ante* actuarial cost to workers.[3] Thus, such a payment is worth much less to workers than its expected cost to firms. In this sense, it acts as a tax on labor and leads to suboptimal employment. It is a payment by firms that creates little value to workers and acts as a wedge, reducing employment below the efficient level.

---

[2]See Dickens 1990 for an exposition of this view. Nicholas A. Ashford and Robert F. Stone (1991, pp. 386–87) argue both that the willingness to pay values are appropriate and that chemical workers are not paid enough *ex ante* to compensate for on-the-job risks. This is inconsistent: either workers are compensated for risks, or the figures are meaningless.

[3]Since death on the job is only a small fraction of all deaths, workers would not rationally reduce their life insurance because of this possible payment. Work-related deaths are only 0.5 percent of all deaths; National Safety Council 1989, pp. 2, 8.

Michael J. Moore and W. Kip Viscusi (1990) and Viscusi (1991) show that the merit rating component of workers' compensation also provides substantial safety incentives. Employers cannot be sued by injured workers. Many injured workers, however, now sue manufacturers of products (such as construction equipment or power tools) involved in workplace accidents. Indeed, such suits are a significant fraction of all product liability claims.

Product Safety

A similar analysis applies to products and product liability. Some studies of willingness to pay are based on behavior in product markets, rather than labor markets (Miller 1990, p. 27). So again, the calculation of a measure of willingness to pay for prevention assumes that appropriate precautions are already provided by market forces. The calculation assumes that consumers are already compensated for bearing risk, in the sense of paying higher prices for goods that incorporate reduced risk. As with workplace safety, the use of hedonic values for deterrence leads to efficient precautions only if the market provides no other mechanisms for inducing such precautions. But the market does provide additional mechanisms, particularly with contractual relationships between firms and consumers.

The simplest mechanism is reputation. Product-related deaths are extremely costly to firms. Indeed, there is evidence that mere failure to take safety precautions, even independently of unfortunate outcomes, is enough to impose substantial costs on firms. Much of the evidence on safety comes from event studies of the effects of safety-related incidents on the value of firms. These studies, based on modern theories of efficient capital markets, rely on examination of stock prices to determine the effects of various events on the value of firms. The findings indicate a substantial cost to firms from events involving harm to consumers, or even risks of harms. The stock market measures the loss in value of reputation to a firm from making or being accused of making an unsafe product.[4]

Some studies have examined recalls related to safety (Peltzman

---

[4]The findings apply directly to firms large enough to have stock traded on organized exchanges, but there is no reason to expect that other firms would not suffer similar, if unmeasured, losses in reputation value.

and Jarrell 1985; Rubin, Murphy, and Jarrell 1988). This literature finds that, for products recalled by the FDA and for products recalled by the CPSC, there are substantial effects on the stock value of the firms involved, even though many of the involved risks are quite small. The cost to firms of the recalls appears to be significantly larger than any plausible measure of the likely direct cost of the recall or of the cost of associated liability. The necessary inference is that there is a large reputation cost to having a product recalled. This reputation cost is a measure of the reduced value that consumers place on the products of the firm.[5]

Mark Mitchell (1989) finds that product tampering has a significant effect on the stock prices of manufacturers involved, again indicating a cost in reputation to firms involved.[6] This result applies even though there is no realistic method that firms could have used to prevent the tampering.

Perhaps of most direct relevance is the analysis by W. Kip Viscusi and Joni Hersch (1990) of product liability actions. They find that news stories reporting on product liability suits and on regulatory events lead to significant losses in a firm's stock value. Losses are greater when personal injury is involved. Again, the magnitude of losses is significant and indicates a large cost to firms from allegations involving product safety. Yet these large losses apparently are imposed by public reaction to the existence of an injury, not by the prospect of losses in court.

John D. Graham (1991) has also argued that reputation effects associated with product liability litigation are quite significant in inducing additional expenditures on safety in the motor vehicle industry. He concludes:

> Interestingly, our cases suggest that the indirect effect of liability—operating through adverse publicity about a product's safety and a manufacturer's reputation—is often the most significant contribution of liability to safety. The direct financial

---

[5]Sam Peltzman and Greg Jarrell found a similar effect for auto recalls, but George E. Hoffer, Stephen W. Pruitt, and Robert J. Reilly (1988) indicate that this was erroneous.

[6]There is also a literature finding that airline crashes lead to losses in the value of associated firms (for example, Mitchell and Maloney 1989), but others dispute these findings (for example, Borenstein and Zimmerman 1988).

costs of liability are usually a relatively minor factor, at least from the perspective of large manufacturers. (pp.181–82)

Graham finds similar results in his statistical analysis: NHTSA regulation, proportion of vehicle miles on interstate highways, consumer income (a measure of demand for safety), and unemployment (a measure of the business cycle) were all significant in explaining reduced highway deaths, but liability (measured in several alternative ways) was not.[7]

Since firms do suffer these large losses in value because of safety problems, there is no reason to assume that the only sanction for production of unsafe products is that associated with the tort system. On the contrary, consumers apparently reduce their demand for products alleged or proved to be unsafe. This decision provides substantial market incentives for firms to produce safe products and reduces or eliminates the need for damage payments to provide safety incentives.

To the extent that tort litigation provides information to markets regarding the safety of products, damage payments should be sufficiently large to make such litigation worthwhile for plaintiffs. Parents sending children to camp, for example, might want an implicit insurance policy from the camp of, say, $100,000. The parents would not want the money after the child's death, for insurance purposes. Rather, the policy would indicate to the camp that the court system would be involved after a death, so that the camp would have an incentive to take efficient precautions. Any additional payment, however, such as for hedonic or other extraordinary damages, or large payments for pain and suffering, serve no efficiency purpose. Moreover, as indicated in chapter 6, there are additional large efficiency losses from such payments.

Punitive Damages

In recent years, consumers have been increasingly able to obtain punitive damage awards in product liability cases. Punitive damage payments traditionally have been available only if the misconduct of

---

[7]Alcohol consumption and average recorded speed were significant in leading to increased fatalities. Robert W. Crandall (1991) does not find Graham's analysis dispositive on the effect of liability on automobile safety.

the injurer was egregious. Some critics of the tort system believe, however, that this form of award is now too easily obtained. The only purpose of this form of damages is deterrence; by definition, punitive damage payments are above and beyond any damage payments needed for compensation. Since some forms of behavior might not be adequately deterred by the mechanisms discussed so far, there is some room for punitive damage payments. Consumers, however, would want to return to a standard of severe limitations for this form of damage award.

A reasonable standard might be that punitive damage payments would be available only if the underlying conduct rose to the level of criminal behavior. Such damage payment would be particularly appropriate if it could be shown that the firm made an explicit attempt to conceal the danger from consumers. In this case, damage payments might be a multiple of injury costs in order to induce firms not to attempt such concealment. The standard of proof, however, should probably approach the standard required for a criminal conviction, with the burden of proof on the plaintiff, before such damage payments should be allowed.

Summary

If tort law were the only force in society for safety, then large damage payments might be efficient. There are, however, numerous other forces for safety. One is direct government regulation of safety. Virtually no product or service escapes such regulation, and the products likely to be involved in tort litigation are extensively regulated. Indeed, for an important class of products, pharmaceuticals, evidence indicates excessive regulation, so additional regulation imposed by tort law is clearly unneeded. Virtually all other products are regulated in one way or another.

In addition, there is no reason to assume complete consumer ignorance of risks, which is the assumption required for hedonic damage payments to be efficient. The data used to calculate hedonic payments assume that wages reflect risk, so such payments are not needed for workplace safety and would lead to excessive spending on safety and to not enough workers being hired, both measured from the perspective of workers themselves.

There is also evidence that consumers of products respond to safety problems. Recalls and product liability litigation lead to large losses in the value of firms. These losses may be interpreted as responses to information about safety. This implies that an important function of tort law may be the provision of information about the safety of products but that damage payments need only be sufficiently large to provide an incentive for litigation.

In chapter 4, I indicated the sorts of damage payments that consumers would likely specify contractually if they were free to do so. Payments at this level would likely provide adequate incentives for information generating litigation without leading to excessive costs of products. They would thus serve to provide both adequate compensation and adequate incentives for safety. In chapter 6, we see that larger damage payments have substantial costs to consumers.

6

Effects of Large
Damage Payments

The analysis in this chapter deals with nonpecuniary damage payments, such as awards for pain and suffering or for lost pleasure of life.[1] The elements at issue in litigation regarding the level of payments for such damages are obviously not traded in any market; there is no explicit market price for injury or for death. Thus, there is no obvious way in which juries can decide the proper dollar amount for such damage payments. This creates uncertainty about the likely outcome of a trial, and uncertainty is one factor making litigation more likely (Cooter and Rubinfeld 1989). One benefit of eliminating this form of damage payment is the reduced likelihood of litigation. (This is also a major benefit of scheduling the payment of this type of damage payment, as discussed by Bovberg, Sloan, and Blumstein [1989].)

A proposal for measuring such damages is receiving some attention from the courts. This concern the use of hedonic or willingness-to-pay damages.[2] This measure of damages is based on linear extrapolations of wage premiums demanded by workers to accept risky jobs. If a job has a 1 in 1,000 chance of death per year, for example, and pays $2,000 more per year than a comparable job without this risk, then the value of life associated with this job is $2 million. Economists at regulatory agencies routinely use these values in making safety decisions.[3] Even though it

---

[1]For a similar analysis, see Calfee and Rubin 1992 and Rubin and Calfee 1992.

[2]This proposal is discussed in Bodine 1992; Dickens 1990; Havrilesky 1990; Miller 1989, 1990; Rubin 1989; Rubin and Calfee 1992; Smith 1990; and Viscusi 1990.

[3]I used these values when I was chief economist at the Consumer Product Safety Commission. See Rodgers and Rubin 1989.

may be desirable to use such values for *ex ante* safety regulation, however, it is not desirable to use them for *ex post* compensation, for the reasons discussed at length in chapter 4.

While the arguments made so far indicate that tort law is inefficient, if this theory of damage payments is adopted by the courts, the degree of inefficiency will greatly increase. James A. Henderson and Aaron D. Twerski (1991A, B) argue that tort rules have reached their logical extreme and that strict liability without fault is not possible. Even if rules do not change, however, the law may become more inefficient as a result of increased damage payments. In particular, hedonic damage payments are receiving increased use in the courtroom. One use of such damage payments has recently been allowed by the Supreme Court, as discussed in chapter 1.[4] If this theory becomes settled law, then damage payments will greatly increase, and the already observed harmful effects of tort law will be exacerbated. While Henderson and Twerski may be correct in arguing that legislatures will ultimately limit damage payments, nonetheless, if this theory is adopted, there will be substantial costs during the period before such legislation can be passed. Henderson and Twerski do not directly address this theory of damage payments.

Viscusi (1991, p. 109) estimates that this measure of damages will increase damage payments for wrongful death by about ten times. This estimate is based on a sample of workers with a value of life estimated at $6.4 million. For this sample of workers, the present value of future earnings would be about $500,000.[5] If we take the latter figure as the estimated pecuniary losses, then awarding the figures for the value of life would imply an increase in damage payments of more than ten times. Actual damage payments now are less than future earnings but sometimes include some nonpecuniary payments. Thus, an estimate of an increase in damage payments of ten times should be a reasonable approximation.

If hedonic damages or other large payments for nonpecuniary losses such as pain and suffering simply failed to provide efficient insurance and deterrence, that would be sufficient reason not to encourage systematic use of such damage payments. But hedonic damage payments also induce price distortions, which bring further

---

[4]Molzof v. U.S., 90–838, 60 U.S.L.W. 4081 (January 14, 1992).

[5]Data in 1980 dollars.

costs. Indeed, current tort law has already introduced substantial distortions, and the new theory would only exacerbate this problem.

Product price serves two functions in the context of product liability and safety. One, the more general function, is simply to allocate resources. The other, more specific to the role of liability, is to provide a signal of the level of risk associated with using a product. The product liability system (particularly in the form of strict liability) has often been justified as making product price more useful for both these functions—at least when losses are pecuniary (for example, Shavell 1987). Imposition of damage payments for nonpecuniary losses, however, introduces distortions that render price inefficient under strict liability from the standpoint of both resource allocation and risk assessment.

Price and Resource Allocation

The allocation problem arises from the bundling of unwanted insurance with products. Product price must increase to cover the involuntary insurance premium, and, given the administrative and other inefficiencies bound to inhere in insurance provided through tort liability, the cost of such a policy will substantially exceed its actuarial value. The policy is essentially worthless to buyers. Parents would be willing to pay essentially zero for a multimillion dollar life insurance policy on a child going off to summer camp, and a worker would place a low value on an additional multimillion dollar life insurance policy on his own life. Therefore, the premium for this involuntary insurance is more or a less a deadweight loss added to product price.

This cost increase will distort consumer choices. Risks associated with some activities (which I call background risks) are not covered by the liability system, and so prices for these activities will not reflect any cost of unwanted insurance. If a child playing at home is killed in an accident (non-product related), for example, there is no liability. If a child drowns at summer camp, the camp will likely be liable. Even if the odds of death at a summer camp are only 1 in 100,000, a $5 million insurance policy would cost $50, plus the cost of administrative inefficiencies. This could lead some parents to keep a child at home, even though camp may be no riskier, and perhaps even safer, than playing at home in the backyard. Where the odds of injury are greater, market effects can be striking. Examples are light

60

airplanes (whose sales have been greatly reduced; Priest 1992), diving boards of municipal swimming pools (which have almost disappeared), and football helmets (where some manufacturers have exited the market).

Perhaps the clearest examples of price distortions occur in connection with products that, while risky, actually decrease the consumer's exposure to risk. Many products subject to potential tort liability serve to reduce risk. Medical care, for example, reduces risk but is subject to malpractice liability. Before kidney dialysis, patients died from kidney failure but could not sue. Since this technology has become available, patients live longer, but there are many opportunities for suit (Tancredi and Nelkin 1991, p. 254). Pharmaceuticals also generally reduce risks but are associated with liability. Terence Dungworth (1988) indicates that 13.5 percent of all product liability cases in his sample are pharmaceuticals. Huber (1985) has argued persuasively that many products governed by the tort system are risk reducing. Development of an AIDS vaccine is being slowed by fears of liability (Cohen 1992).

Many of the more prominent tort cases involve risk-reducing products. Many alleged injuries caused by asbestos, a fire retardent, occurred during World War II, when it was being installed in warships to increase their safety. Agent Orange was a defoliant used in Vietnam to eliminate hiding places that could have been used to attack the soldiers who later alleged harm from the chemical. DES was used to prevent miscarriages; many of those harmed by the drug would not have been born without it. The Bjork-Shiley Convexo-Concave heart valve reduced danger from blood clots but sometimes fractured. Pfizer, its manufacturer, has developed a newer valve that does not fracture, the firm sells the device abroad but not in the United States, partly because of a fear of liability (Tancredi and Nelkin 1991, pp. 260–61).

Further evidence is provided by an examination of the behavior to the Association of Trial Lawyers of America, an organization of plaintiffs' tort lawyers. One of their functions is provision of a basis for organizing litigation groups, "voluntary networks of ATLA members sharing an interest in a particular type of case" (ATLA n.d.). There are forty-seven broad groups (some with subgroups). Many of these groups deal clearly with risk-reducing or health-increasing goods or services: Accutane (an anti-acne medication); Agent Orange; AIDS litigation; air bag and seat belt failures; birth defects (including Bendectin); birth trauma; Chymopapain (a chemical used for spinal problems); Dalkon shield; DES; DPT vaccine; IUDs (general); nonsteroidal antiinflammatory drugs (often used in treatment of arthritis); nursing homes; and tardive dyskinesia (a side effect of treatment for schizophrenia).

For products that reduce risk, the large damage payments associated with payments for nonpecuniary losses can actually lead to consumers facing increased risk. Again, background risks (for example, the risk of dying from a disease if there is no medical or pharmaceutical intervention, of being shot by a Viet Cong, of being involuntary aborted and hence never born) are not associated with the costs of involuntary insurance.

Consider a hypothetical case of a vaccine that reduces the risk of a fatal illness and entails pecuniary losses of $10,000 and nonpecuniary losses of death valued at $5 million (to use a typical figure from Viscusi 1990). Risk of injury without the vaccine is .0015, and risk when using the product is .0010 (a one-third reduction in risk). The average and marginal costs of producing the vaccine taking optimal care is $10.[6]

Under a regime of no liability (but with optimal precautions), the competitive price of the vaccine is $10. Under strict liability for monetary damages only, price is $10 + .001($10,000) = $10 + $10 = $20, reflecting the .0010 probability of having to pay out $10,000, if the product fails. The value to consumers of the prevention offered by the vaccine is the reduction in monetary losses (estimated as .0005 × $10,000 = $5) plus the amount consumers would have paid for the marginal .0005 reduction in the probability of death (.0005 × $5,000,000 = $2,500), a total of $2,505. If consumer perceptions of relative risks are anywhere close to the truth, consumers will correctly choose to use the vaccine because its benefits of $2,505 greatly exceed its costs of $20.

Now add damage payments for hedonic losses. Price increases by $5,000, reflecting the .0010 chance of making a liability payment of $5 million, for a total price of $5,020. But consumer willingness to pay for the prevention offered by the vaccine is only $2,505. It seems unlikely that consumers would wish to pay anything close to the extra $2,515 for a lottery that awards $5 million in the event of death (the extreme

---

[6]I assume prevention expenditures are approximately at the optimal level or at least at a level sufficient to make the product useful. One could argue that this is necessary for the vaccine to gain approval of physicians and the FDA.

reduction in marginal utility of wealth). Rather, informed consumers would choose not to use the vaccine and instead would live with the greater risk associated with no protection at all. Thus liability would tend to defeat even the preferences of informed consumers. At $5,020, the vaccine costs more than its worth to consumers who are fully aware of the risk of not using the vaccine.

A situation much like the one outlined here may obtain in fact. Recent news reports (for example, *New York Times*, August 28, 1990, p. D2) on the drug Chlozaril, a powerful treatment for schizophrenia, indicate that approximately a .0002 probability of fatal side effects has led to extremely thorough field monitoring and a high price of about $9,000 per year. Both of these problems are apparently absent in European markets, in which it is unlikely that fatal side effects will lead to large liability payments. There seem to be instances in which the drug is not used because of the price. Legislation has been introduced to permit Medicaid to purchase the drug without paying for the monitoring program. (This situation has recently been resolved as a result of pressure from the FTC and others, so that a single provider is no longer required for testing of drug users. Whether a similar resolution has been achieved regarding potential liability exposure for the manufacturer remains to be seen.)

In circumstances such as these, the risk-reducing product must reduce risk by at least one-half to be sold. Essentially, the consumer must pay twice for the risk: once for the remaining risk itself, again for the (unwanted) insurance policy against pain and suffering. In the above example, if the vaccine reduced the risk by half, from .0015 to .00075, then the value to consumers of the product would be approximately $3,750 (.00075 × $5,000,000), and the cost would also be approximately $3,750. For products that reduce risk by less than this amount, however, even fully informed consumers who value the product at much more than its true cost of production can be discouraged from consumption.

When risk is greater than marginal—as with emergency services for the critically injured—the effects of liability for hedonic damages can be even stronger. A product or service that increases the probability of surviving from 1 percent to 5 percent (still leaving a 95 percent chance of death), for example, could encounter pricing problems so severe as to price the good out of the market, even if the provider has only a relatively small chance of actually being found liable.

There is another mechanism through which increased damage payments can increase risk. Firms may seek ways to avoid such damage payments. One way is to incorporate risky activities in relatively small firms that have little to lose from bankruptcy. This is already occurring (Ringleb and Wiggins 1990; Wiggins and Ringleb 1992). As damage payments become larger, however, this behavior can be increased. Henderson and Twerski (1991A,B) indicate that, as firms begin to assume that they will become bankrupt rather than pay damages from tort litigation, then they will reduce precautions, thus leading to increased risk.

In sum, consumers generally do not wish to acquire insurance against nonpecuniary losses, including pain and suffering and lost future pleasure of life. If tort law awards such damage payments, then product price will increase to reflect the actuarial cost of this unwanted insurance. This action will increase product price to such a level that many consumers will choose not to purchase desired products. In the special case of risk-reducing products, the effect can be to impose greater risk on consumers. Greater risk can also occur as firms plan on bankruptcy and therefore reduce precautions against risk. In the next section, I present some actual examples.

Some Examples

When a manufacturer of a relatively but not absolutely safe product is found liable for some injury that occurs with the product, then the price of this product relative to relatively safer alternatives will increase. This price increase and any adverse publicity generated by the damage payment (as discussed in chapter 5) will shift consumers to the use of more dangerous products.

In theory, the law recognizes this problem for some classes of products. Comment K of the Uniform Restatement of Torts, Second, applies to "unavoidably unsafe products," as discussed in Henderson and Twerski 1987. This has generally been applied to drugs. Even here, however, there has been excessive liability on drug manufacturers. There is evidence, for example, that increased liability costs imposed on vaccine manufacturers have led to reduced vaccinations and increased risks. For many major vaccines, only one manufacturer now exists, since other producers have exited the market, in part because of liability fears.

Louis Lasagna (1991, pp. 341–45) discusses the effects of litigation on vaccines in detail and also on orphan drugs. Laurence Tancredi and Dorothy Nelkin (1991, p. 259) also discuss vaccines and indicate that Genentech has ceased development of a potential AIDS vaccine because of a fear of malpractice liability. They also indicate that, as of 1988, only one company was engaged in contraception research, although at least thirteen companies had engaged in this research in the 1970s. Edmund W. Kitch (1985) also discusses vaccines.

The argument applies to any product that reduces risk without eliminating it. There are many examples.

In *Campbell v. General Motors*,[7] GM was found liable for a design defect in a bus. The death rate on transit buses, however, is so low as to be virtually unmeasurable (National Safety Council 1986, p. 77). Increasing the costs of bus rides, as would occur from decisions placing liability on buses, would shift some riders from buses to cars and increase general social risk; the extent of the increase would depend on the price increase and the elasticity of demand.[8] A similar argument applies to airplanes. When a plane crashes, large damage payments are routine. We know that planes are fifty times as safe as cars (on a per-passenger mile basis; NSC 1986, p. 77), but there is no large compensation for most auto-related deaths. These large damage payments for airplane accidents raise airfares (not by much, since accidents are rare) and therefore shift some passengers from planes to cars. The predictable result is more deaths (as discussed in another context by Sam Kazman [1991]).

O'Brien v. Muskin,[9] New Jersey, 1983 involved a diving accident in an aboveground pool. The issue as litigated was feasible alternative designs. This case was notable for a new and inefficient standard of design defect (Larsen 1984). Another point, however, is that Consumer Product Safety Commission data show that aboveground pools are safer

---

[7]Campbell v. General Motors Corp., 32 Cal. 3d 112, 649 P.2d, 184 Cal. Rptr., 891 (1982), reprinted in Henderson and Twerski 1987, p. 545.

[8]Liability in this decision was found because there was no handle for a passenger on the first seat in the bus to grab. Washington, D.C., subways also lack such a handle; the decision does not seem to have led to major design changes.

[9]O'Brien v. Muskin Corp., 94 N.J. 169, 463 A.2d 298 (1983), reprinted in Henderson and Twerski 1987, p. 551.

with respect to child drowning than in-ground pools; increased liability for design defects in the former will increase at least some classes of risk. There have been recent cases of liability placed on manufacturers of disposable lighters. Lighters are safer than matches; imposition of liability will again increase risk (see Rubin 1987).

Particularly tragic is the situation involving obstetrics and prenatal care. For many of the poor, infant mortality rates are actually rising, and in general the rate of decrease has greatly slowed. There are many causes for this, but at least part of the problem is the unwillingness of many obstetricians to accept Medicaid patients, partly because of a fear of malpractice suits (Nazario 1988). In the District of Columbia, 80 percent of all obstetricians have been sued. As a result, many obstetricians are moving their practices to the suburbs around Washington, denying care particularly to the poor (Epps 1989). Stanley Joel Reiser (1991, pp. 240–41) indicates that, as of 1987, 12.4 percent of U.S. OB-GYN physicians had given up obstetrics, and 27 percent had decreased high-risk care. In many states, family practitioners had ceased delivering babies, so that many mothers were required to drive long distances for care.

There are other ways in which inappropriate liability can increase risk. In a well-known, 1978 case in California, *Barker v. Lull*,[10] plaintiff was operating a high-lift loader and fell, receiving serious injuries. From the facts, it seems clear that the plaintiff, Barker, was unskilled in operating the equipment that caused the injury, and in fact the equipment was being operated in an area where a crane, a substitute machine, would have been more appropriate. The court found for Barker. The desirable solution (to reduce costs of both accidents and avoidance) would have been for Barker to take more care. That is, it is more efficient to have both cranes and high-lift loaders available, with the former used in rough terrain. It is also efficient for inexperienced operators to refuse to operate a piece of equipment in dangerous terrain. (In fact, the normal operator did refuse to work on the day in question, for just this reason.)

The economic theory of liability indicates that it is efficient for liability to be placed on the low-cost avoider. Shifting liability to high-cost avoiders has perverse safety effects, in addition to the extra

---

[10]Barker v. Lull Engineering Co., 20 Cal. 3d 413, 573 P. 2d 443, 143 Cal. Rptr. 225 (1978), reprinted in Henderson and Twerski 1987, p. 531.

costs mentioned above. If workers believe that they will be compensated for injuries, they will be less likely to take care, where care consists in things like not operating machinery without training or in dangerous conditions. It may seem that the risk of physical injury is enough to offer adequate deterrence, but theory and data both show that money payments, such as expected liability payments, can increase risky behavior. The result is likely to be reduced safety.

Barker is notable also for a remarkable argument that seems to be dicta, but which the court relied on in shifting the burden of proof in a risk-utility balancing case from plaintiff to defendant:

> The technological revolution has created a society that contains dangers to the individual never before contemplated. The individual must face the threat to life and limb not only from the car on the street or highway, but from a massive array of hazardous mechanisms and products. The radical change from a comparatively safe, largely agricultural, society to this industrial unsafe one has been reflected in the decisions that formerly tied liability to the fault of a tortfeasor but now are more concerned with the safety of the individual who suffers the loss. (Quoted in Henderson and Twerski 1987, pp. 540–41)

This language was unanimously agreed to by six judges. This is remarkable in that the premises of the statement are factually incorrect. Agriculture is and has been among the most dangerous occupations. In 1985, agriculture was 30 percent more risky than construction, and eight times as risky as manufacturing.[11] Moreover, all data show that our industrial, unsafe society is vastly safer than any previous society.[12] Thus, in *Barker*, the court imposed a new burden of proof, based solely on an erroneous reading of the statistical or historical record.[13]

---

[11]NSC (1986, p. 23), indicates that annual death rates per 100,000 workers are forty-nine in agriculture, thirty-seven in construction, and six in manufacturing.

[12]From 1930 to 1985, for examples, life expectancy at birth increased from sixty to seventy-five years. Work accident deaths have gone from fifteen to five per 100,000 population. Home accident death rates and death rates per 100 million vehicle miles have also fallen radically (NSC 1986, cited in Rubin 1987).

[13]In general, people believe that the world has become more dangerous, even though all data (such as that in the previous note) show that it has become safer. Seventy-eight percent of the public believes that the world is more dangerous now than twenty years ago, Crouch and Wilson 1982, p. 3. Substantial decisions are based on such erroneous data.

Walter Olson (1988) provides numerous plausible (though not empirically tested) examples of increasing risk from inappropriate liability. (Claims that tort law reduces risk are not empirically tested, either.) Some of these examples are reformulation of pharmaceuticals at lower but less effective dosages; seatbelts without slack, which are safer when used but used less because they are less comfortable; purchase of smaller and more dangerous automobiles as a result of price increases;[14] retention of less safe cars longer as prices of new cars increase (and similarly of other products); replacement of safer day care centers with unlicensed day care providers with no liability exposure; and in general more do-it-yourself activity as the cost of market activities increases.

Priest (1988 and elsewhere) has argued that there is no evidence that the explosion in tort litigation has caused increased safety. This lack is not surprising, because the evidence, as presented above, is at least as consistent with a claim that tort law has led to reduced, not increased, safety.

Price and Risk Signaling

An entirely different problem is the relationship between product price and perceived risk. Strict liability for pecuniary losses tends to induce a price that reflects total costs of the product, including risk (ignoring the usual inefficiencies in running an insurance program through the liability system). The price of the product includes the expected cost of the pecuniary losses associated with the product, since manufacturers will be forced to pay consumers this amount under strict liability.

This relationship completely fails to hold when losses are nonpecuniary, or irreplaceable. Several factors lead to the breakdown of the relationship between price and risk for nonpecuniary losses.

Consider, first, large probabilities of large losses. If the injury is so severe that potential victims would be willing to pay substantial amounts to reduce risk, the damage payment extrapolated from willingness to pay for a marginal reduction in risk is greater (perhaps much greater) than actual willingness to pay to eliminate the risk altogether. That is, a consumer might be willing to pay $100,000

---

[14]Or, as Sam Kazman (1991) has stressed, because of CAFE gasoline economy standards.

(perhaps his entire net worth) to reduce a risk of death from 51 percent to 50 percent. The consumer would not (because he could not) pay $5 million, however, to reduce the risk to zero. Essentially, this is an income effect. It is in this sense that the extrapolated figures overstate willingness to pay to eliminate the risk. As a result, prices under strict liability actually tend to overstate total costs, including risk. As shown above, even fully informed consumers would make inefficient choices in the face of such prices.

If risks are marginal, then the price including expected hedonic damage payments tends to reflect full social costs (in the sense of including a willingness-to-pay measure of the costs of risks involved in using the product). But great inefficiencies remain nonetheless. For one thing, prices and the associated bundled insurance misallocate wealth from consumers with high marginal utility of income (those who have not been injured) to consumers with low marginal utility of wealth (victims). Parents with surviving children will be relatively poorer, and parents who have lost children will be relatively wealthier. Clearly, this situation is inferior to one in which price is equal to cost of production and full risk information is available to consumers.

An even more fundamental problem arises when we consider how consumers would use these risk-adjusted prices to distinguish among products of various degrees and kinds of risk. Compensation for pecuniary losses leaves consumers whole, so that with complete compensation victims are indifferent between the occurrence and the nonoccurrence of accidents. This cannot be true of nonpecuniary losses. By its nature, any level of compensation for severe nonpecuniary losses leaves consumers under-compensated. The buyer of a product involving nonpecuniary risk would therefore be willing to pay toward reducing that risk, even though all cost-justified precautions have been taken. That is, the remaining risk represents a true loss in utility to the consumer even though there is no cost-effective way of reducing this risk. This remaining risk represents a latent cost of the product, over and above the monetary cost, and price cannot reflect this cost.

Buyers cannot use price as a full proxy for risk. (The same argument applies in the workplace context.) The price induced by hedonic damage payments would not support accurate utility comparisons among products that do or do not cause pain and suffering or among products that involve different kinds of suffering. In particular, consumers would not be alerted to the superiority of products that cause only pecuniary losses (which would be preferred, because they can be efficiently insured against).

As an example, consider the choice between two home furnaces. Both are prone to failure, with a probability of .01, but in different ways. One could destroy a home, at a purely monetary cost of $100,000, while the other could cause an illness so severe that the user would pay $100,000 (almost his entire wealth) to prevent it. If a failure occurred, the user of the first would be fully compensated by the $100,000 insurance payment, but the user of the second would not. Therefore, consumers would prefer to purchase the first if they were aware of the nature of the risks. Clearly, price competition, even under strict liability, would not facilitate efficient choices by consumers. Both products would carry an implicit insurance premium of $1,000 (.01 × $100,000), but the risk-adjusted prices would provide no clue as to the difference between the two kinds of losses.

Thus the price induced by hedonic damage payments often has the paradoxical property of overstating social cost and understating consumer cost. The reason is the disparity between willingness to pay for prevention and willingness to pay for insurance. With such a disparity, insurance cannot be a perfect substitute (perhaps not even a good substitute) for risk information. When price includes the insurance premium induced by hedonic damage payments, the effect is not to convey risk information accurately. Rather, the effect is to dissuade efficient purchases by informed consumers, yet fail to dissuade inefficient purchases by uninformed consumers.

These price distortions arise with special force with products that reduce risk. The distortions can occur even when the products involved are not inherently risky. Some products, such as day care facilities or summer camps, may do no more than transfer an existing risk from self-insurance (because no purchased product or service is involved) to partial insurance through the tort system. If tort liability includes hedonic damage payments, the effect can be, again, significantly distorted prices and, consequently, less efficient consumer decisions.

Summary

Use of damage payments based on willingness-to-pay estimates for value of life would greatly increase the magnitude of tort damage payments for wrongful death. There is no theoretical justification for such an increase. Theory and evidence indicate that consumers do not desire the increased insurance against nonpecuniary losses associated with such large damage payments. There is no evidence that risk-imposing behavior is underdeterred. Indeed, the data used to calculate hedonic values imply that, in workplace accidents, *ex ante* payments for risk are adequate to provide proper incentives. Substantial evidence indicates that markets impose a high cost for inflicting risk from products on consumers.

Since these payments are not needed for deterrence and are not valued by consumers at their actuarial cost as insurance, the use of such damage measures would induce a large price distortion in the marketplace. This would be particularly troublesome for products that reduce risk; under plausible scenarios, informed consumers could be discouraged from buying products whose value is substantially greater than costs, unless risk is reduced by at least 50 percent. Consumers are forced to pay for the unwanted insurance, which is bundled with the product.

Some economists argue that prices that include damage payments can signal risk to consumers, since consumers must explicitly pay for the risk. This justification is approximately correct for pecuniary damages. For nonpecuniary damages, however, it fails. It is possible to compensate consumers fully for pecuniary losses, but it is not possible for nonpecuniary losses. Therefore, insured consumers would prefer a product that causes $\$X$ in expected pecuniary losses over a product that causes $\$X$ in expected nonpecuniary losses. Price of the product, however, cannot signal this difference; the bundled insurance premium for both types of risk would be the same. Therefore, price cannot provide the information regarding relative risk and types of risk that is sometimes thought to be an advantage of the tort system.

Thus, large payments for hedonic losses or for pain and suffering serve no useful function. They are not needed for deterrence. They provide unwanted insurance. They do not provide useful information regarding product risk.

71

7
Is a Contractual Solution Feasible?

Many believe that there is no possibility of a contractual solution to problems of excess liability.[1] That is, many, including numerous attorneys, believe that the courts will not accept any contractual limitation on liability. As Havighurst (1986), in his discussion of obstacles to malpractice reform, indicates, "Not the least of these obstacles is the natural conservatism of lawyers who, in counseling health care providers, tend immediately to discount the possibility that tort rights might effectively be altered by private agreement" (p. 144).

It is true that, in several cases, the courts have invalidated contracts limiting liability for malpractice. Two leading cases are *Tunkl v. Regents of the University of California* and *Emory University v. Porubiansky*.[2] In *Tunkl*, a patient had signed a release with the UCLA Medical Center, absolving the center of any liability, including negligent liability; the clause was held to be against public policy by the California Supreme Court. In *Emory*, the contract was between a patient and the Emory University Dental Clinic; in return for lower cost care, the patient had signed an exculpatory clause, absolving the clinic for all liability. The Georgia Supreme Court ruled that this contract was against public policy.

---

[1] Much of this chapter is based on Havighurst 1986 and Ginsburg et al. 1986. These analyses apply to medical malpractice, which is only one element of my proposal. Many of the same legal arguments, however, apply in a broader context. Moreover, as seen below, malpractice may be one of the easiest places to begin implementing the proposals suggested here.

[2] 60 Cal. 2d 92, 383 P. 2d 441, 32 Cal. Rptr. (1963); 248 Ga. 391 S.E. 2d 903 (1981).

In these cases, the contract was a complete exculpation for all liability and damages. As Ginsburg and others (1986) indicate, "The contracts provided no alternative means of assessing liability, imposed no burden on the provider in the event of negligence, and offered no other assurance to the patient against the adverse consequences of the provider's negligence" (p. 254). The contracts proposed here, which eliminate damage payments for nonpecuniary losses, differ in several significant respects from the contracts disallowed by the courts.

These proposed contracts do not exculpate providers of all blame. They do not, for example, allow negligence. Indeed, the type of damage payment limitation that I am proposing does not in any way attempt to change the legal standard for liability. Providers of goods and services would be tried under whatever legal standards applied to the relevant activity (strict liability, negligence, etc.), and the standard of proof would not be modified by contract.

Courts have in fact accepted contracts that limit liability of medical care providers. *Colton v. New York Hospital* upheld a covenant not to sue in a case regarding an experimental medical procedure.[3] In *Schneider v. Revici*, the court upheld an express assumption of risk, even though the treatment used was admittedly unconventional (and, ultimately, ineffective).[4] These limitations of liability go to the issue of the standard of care and therefore may be more problematic than contracts affecting only levels of damage payments.

Ginsburg and others (1986, pp. 253–54) discuss in detail the rationales provided by the courts for failing to enforce contracts limiting malpractice damage awards. The contracts proposed here satisfy many of the critiques suggested by the courts. Moreover, I indicate specific ways in which the contracts can be implemented to alleviate expressed concerns further.

The refusal of the courts to enforce exculpatory contracts in injury cases is a legal anomaly. In general, courts do uphold contracts that are voluntarily signed. Priest (1981), for example, describes consumer product warranties for issues other than safety. Business contracts relating to damage issues are generally upheld as well, except that courts will on occasion order *smaller* damages than agreed

---

[3]98 Misc. 2d 957, 414 N.Y.S.2d 866 (N.Y. Sup. Ct. 1979), cited in Mehlman (1990, p. 409).

[4]817 F.2d 987, 989 (2d Cir. 1987), cited in Mehlman (1990, p. 412).

on if the damage payment is held to be a penalty (for example, Rubin 1983, chap. 4). Thus, if the courts should order *larger* than agreed on damages, this decision would be particularly anomalous. U.S. courts uphold the Warsaw Convention in aircraft crashes involving international travel, which limits death payments unless there is willful negligence. Indeed, this may be the closest analogy to the proposal advanced here, because it is an explicit limit on damage payments.

Satisfying Many Legal Concerns

One concern that has been cited is that contractual relaxation of liability would adversely impact on the standard of care.[5] The proposals here would specifically not impact levels or standards of care.

In addition, injured parties would not be left without remedies. On the contrary, it is expected that contracts would compensate injured persons for all (or almost all; see the discussion in chapter 4) of their pecuniary losses. There would be compensation for all lost earnings and for any medical expenses associated with the injury. This feature would eliminate one of the factors cited by Ginsburg and others.[6]

Another class of elements in the legal challenge to contractual limitations is that such contracts reflect unequal bargaining power and that the contractual terms are not negotiated, so that there is no assurance that other health care providers will not adopt similar contracts.[7] While these factors do not carry much weight in economic analysis (for example, Posner, 1992, pp. 115–17), they are apparently important in legal discourse. To have the courts accept the terms suggested here, it will be useful (and perhaps necessary) to alleviate

---

[5]Ginsburg and others (1986, pp. 253–54) indicate that two relevant factors cited by the courts are: "(c) Private agreements should not reduce a health care provider's statutory or ethical duties; (e) Health care providers should not be able to violate prevailing standards of care with impunity." Contractual limits of liability to pecuniary losses would not violate either of these conditions.

[6]The factor that would be eliminated is: "(i) The financial risk of personal injury should be borne by a negligent party when that party is in a much superior economic position to and capable of taking measures to prevent or insure against losses." Again, the proposal here would explicitly not include contractual limitation of damage payments for financial (pecuniary) risk.

[7]Ginsburg et al. 1986, pp. 253–54, factors a, g, and h.

74

any concern regarding unequal bargaining power, unconscionability, and contracts of adhesion.

To alleviate the courts' concerns about such issues, it will be useful first to offer contracts limiting damages in contexts in which there is a real possibility of explicit choice. Initially, the scope for contractual damage imitation will be relatively narrow. There are, however, benefits from this strategy. As seen below, such contracts may cover many important areas of product liability law.

Moreover, damage-limiting contracts may spread from these narrow areas into more of the law. If courts observe consumers freely choosing damage-limiting contracts in situations where courts believe that there is a true explicit choice, then they may begin to realize that there is a true benefit to consumers from such contracts. If courts uphold these contracts in some circumstances, there would be additional benefits. Assume that many consumers choose such contracts when offered an explicit choice. Then, if other consumers in other contexts (say, involving the purchase of a product) were not offered an explicit choice in a contract or warranty that excluded nonpecuniary damages, the courts might accept these contracts.

As I indicated in chapter 1, I view this proposal as a first step toward relying more heavily on contracts in product-related cases. Therefore, if the courts can be persuaded to uphold contracts in some circumstances, then a move to a more sensible, contract-based system may continue.

Areas for Adoption

These contracts may be most easily adopted in four areas: (1) medical malpractice; (2) workplace injuries; (3) purchase of large durables such as automobiles, small aircraft, and homes; and (4) automobile insurance.[8] Small aircraft may actually be the most promising area in which to begin this reform.

Malpractice. It might be relatively easy to adopt contractual damage limitations regarding medical malpractice in some cases. This reform

---

[8]Automobile accidents involve strangers (parties who are not in a contractual relationship) and so are not strictly within the scope of the analysis presented so far. Automobile owners and their insurance companies, however, are in a contractual relationship. As indicated below, there are practical reasons why focusing on this relationship might be a useful early step.

could most easily occur through medical insurance contracts. Reform would be most feasible in cases where insurance was provided through a preferred provider organization or health maintenance organization, since in these cases the insurance company contracts directly with physicians and other providers.

The contracts would take the following form. A company would offer a health insurance plan with two options. Option A would allow litigation under current rules if there were unfavorable medical outcomes. Option B would be cheaper and would allow recovery only for pecuniary losses. The plans would carefully indicate the exact differences and terms. Thus, option B would spell out carefully that, with some unfavorable outcome, consumers could sue only for lost wages and for direct medical expenses needed to correct the injury, but that option B costs $X less than option A. One source in the literature discusses the possibility of contractually specifying liability rules for the Federal Employees Health Benefits Program, essentially for the same reasons advocated here,[9] and also addresses issues relating to the implementation of such a program.

The plans could cover not only medical malpractice but also liability of drug companies for nonpecuniary damages. The medical insurance company could negotiate a reduced price for pharmaceuticals by showing that consumers would have agreed *ex ante* not to sue for nonpecuniary damages from a mishap. Many medical insurance plans already include payment for drugs (commonly with a copayment of perhaps $5), and it would be relatively easy to have option B require a copayment of (say) $5 and option A, a copayment of a higher amount, based on the actuarial cost of the additional cost of nonpecuniary damages, plus the additional expected expense of litigation induced by this larger but less certain payment.[10]

This plan might be particularly workable, since many consumers of health insurance are already able to choose between various plans, and this would be only an additional modification to that currently

---

[9]"Customizing Liability" 1986.

[10]It would be important to have the premium approximate the actuarial value of the savings, because this comparability could be important evidence to the court that the choice was fair and truly reflected the cost to consumers of the insurance against nonpecuniary losses. The savings, however, would include the reduced litigation costs and the reduced number of claims due to the increased certainty and reduced expected value of the claims.

allowed choice. Thus, administratively, this would be a relatively easy plan to implement. Moreover, since courts apparently do not interfere with the terms of freely chosen health insurance plans, it might be particularly likely that they would not eliminate this choice either. Havighurst (1986, p. 166) indicates that courts are already willing to accept contracts which require arbitration of medical malpractice claims.[11] Since each consumer would have explicit contracts to choose among, to the extent that legal dissatisfaction with contractual limits on liability are based on a theory regarding contracts of adhesion, this plan would reduce or eliminate this problem, because there would be explicit choice.

Workplace Injuries. Injuries in the workplace are a second area where contracting would be possible, although more complex than in the medical area. Under current workmen's compensation laws, employers are not liable for injuries on the job, and so a direct contract with an employer would not serve any purpose. (The level of compensation under workmen's compensation is approximately that suggested here, in that only pecuniary damages are covered, and these are covered at a level aimed at reducing moral hazard problems, as discussed in chapter 4. For a discussion, see Viscusi 1991, chap. 9.)

Even though employers are not liable at tort for on-the-job injuries, there is substantial litigation regarding such injuries. Producers of equipment used on the job are liable, under product liability theories, for workplace injuries. Priest (1992, p. 258) indicates that 60 percent of modern product liability judgments arise from workplace injuries. This class of injuries is a significant part of the product liability issue.

Since employers are not directly involved in this litigation, the required contracts would be complex. At a minimum, there would be different types of contracts for machinery and equipment purchased after and before the signing of the contract; it might not be possible to reach such agreements for already purchased items. For new materials, essentially, the contracts would take the form of employers offering workers increased wages, if workers agreed not to sue manufacturers of workplace equipment for the nonpecuniary cost of injuries. Employers

---

[11]Madden v. Kaiser Foundation Hospitals, 17 Cal. 3d 699, 552 p.2d 1178, 131 Cal. Rptr. 882 (1976).

would recoup this wage premium by paying reduced prices for equipment; the price reductions would be financed by the reduced liability exposure of manufacturers. Landes and Posner (1987, p. 282) indicate that there are already contracts where the buyer of a machine agrees to indemnify the seller, if the seller is held liable for personal injury to a user of the machine.

For already purchased equipment, the process would require an extra step. Because of increased transactions costs, the arrangements might not be feasible; if they are feasible, they would probably apply only in cases where a workplace used a substantial amount of equipment produced by one (still solvent) manufacturer. The employer would then negotiate a deal between the manufacturer of the equipment and the workforce, under which workers would give up rights to sue for nonpecuniary damages associated with the manufacturer's products in return for increased wages; the wage increase would be paid for by the manufacturer in the form of a side payment to the employer, in return for the reduced liability.

In either case, the contract would best be negotiated by a union. During negotiations, the amount of the wage premium paid in return for forgoing rights to sue for nonpecuniary damages would need to be made explicit. If there is no union, then it would probably be best for employers to offer specific wage premiums or other benefits to workers who would agree to forgo their rights to sue, so that some workers might not elect the increased compensation and reduced chance for litigation. (If my arguments are correct, most workers would presumably accept the terms.) If the employer unilaterally made the decision for all workers, the legal enforceability of the arrangement would be subject to some doubt. It would probably be best if the first contracts were contracts for new purchases of material and were signed with unionized workplaces.

Major Durables. For certain major durables, prices are sufficiently high so that explicit negotiation over terms of the contract are feasible. Automobile buyers, for example, have an explicit option regarding extended warranties, which are sold separately from the automobile itself. Many new homes are sold with warranties (Weicher 1984). Of particular interest is the market for general aviation (noncommercial airplanes), which has been virtually eliminated by product liability litigation (Priest 1992).

In all these cases, a negotiated contract excluding damages for pain and suffering would seem feasible. In all cases, the price of the product is sufficiently large and negotiations sufficiently complex, so that it would be possible to include an additional contractual term dealing with payments for nonpecuniary damages from a mishap. For houses, the risk might be sufficiently low, so that no such contract would be worthwhile, although builder liability associated with a housing development might be greater. For automobiles, the risks are greater but also perhaps not sufficiently great to make such a contract worthwhile.

For general aviation aircraft, the payoff could be quite substantial. Priest (1992, pp. 259, 262) estimates that insurance costs associated with small aircraft are between $75,000 and $80,000 per plane. He also estimates that unwanted coverage associated with tort liability typically raises costs between 1.64 and 2.34 times the coverage desired by consumers.[12] The price of such aircraft could be lowered by between $32,000 and $49,000, simply by adopting the contractual standard proposed here. The magnitudes in this market are sufficiently great so that this might be the most promising arena in which to attempt contractual tort reform.

Automobile Insurance. Automobile accidents involve parties who are not in a contractual relationship. Consumers and their own insurance companies, however, are in such a relationship. O'Connell (1990) has proposed a plan under which insureds would give up their right to sue for nonpecuniary damages if they were in an accident with another party who had also given up these rights. In this circumstance, rates could be lowered more as more parties agreed to such contracts. He estimates savings between 25 and 50 percent of insurance bills, depending on the type of contracts elected (O'Connell, 1990, p. 951). This proposal is particularly interesting because President Bush proposed a law forcing states to allow consumers to choose such policies. A key part of the law would allow consumers to sign contracts exempting insurance companies from paying damages for pain and suffering.

Such a law would have substantial benefits in its own right. In addition, if it were passed, it could serve as a useful precedent for the

---

[12]Priest 1992, p. 245, n. 36, citing Priest 1987, p. 1556.

proposals advanced here for product liability and medical malpractice insurance. In particular, if many consumers voluntarily agreed to purchase insurance without compensation for pain and suffering, then this decision could be used as evidence that warranties or other disclaimers for such coverage are the result of rational consumer responses, rather than terms forced on powerless consumers.

Summary

Although the conventional wisdom is that courts will not enforce any contracts limiting liability for injuries, there is little legal basis for this belief. Courts have refused to enforce contracts that eliminated all liability, but there has never been a set of cases examining partial elimination of liability. Indeed, under the Warsaw Convention, governing airline deaths in international travel, contracts similar to those advocated here are upheld. Contracts eliminating damage payments for nonpecuniary losses would alleviate many of the concerns expressed by the courts. These contracts would not affect standards of care, and they would not leave injured consumers uncompensated for injuries. Moreover, if they were carefully drafted and if consumers were offered specific choices, then the contracts could not be eliminated as being contracts of adhesion. Two particularly promising areas for writing such agreements are medical malpractice, where many consumers already face a choice of contracts, and general aviation, where such contracts might reduce the cost of small airplanes by up to $50,000.

The analysis in this book has argued that, if consumers had the option, they would typically choose reduced prices and contracts eliminating their ability to sue for nonpecuniary damages. In this chapter, I have argued that there is a good chance that courts would uphold such contracts, if they were presented with the contracts and if drafters were careful in writing and implementing the contracts. It is time to attempt such contracts. The result may be a substantial amount of tort reform without a need for legislation.

Careful drafting would be required. It would be important to correctly specify rights of third parties. If equipment were sold with a warranty disclaiming damages for nonpecuniary losses, for example, then it would be important to be sure that this disclaimer applied to additional users (besides the purchaser) and to subsequent buyers. It

80

would also be necessary to be sure that suppliers of components were not liable if the primary seller were not liable. Good contract lawyers, however, would have no trouble in drafting appropriate provisions to cover these and other contingencies.[13]

---

[13]These issues were raised at a conference at the American Enterprise Institute. Professor Jeffrey O'Connell of the University of Virginia, who has drafted statutes with provisions similar to those proposed here (O'Connell 1981, 1990) provided some immediate suggestions for handling these issues. This book argues for the form of the solution; others are more qualified to provide the necessary details.

8
Summary

This book has provided a modest suggestion for tort reform: parties in contractual relations (manufacturers and consumers, doctors and patients, workers and employers) should be allowed to specify contractually the level of damage payments for injury. This relatively simple policy would have far-reaching beneficial implications for current tort law.

A major benefit of the proposal is that it is a voluntary solution. I suggest terms that parties would probably agree to, if they were allowed to freely contract. In particular, I suggest that parties would agree that injured consumers would be compensated for pecuniary losses (losses that can be replaced by money, such as lost earnings and direct medical costs) but not for nonpecuniary losses (losses that cannot be compensated by money, such as pain and suffering or lost pleasure of life). If the theory on which this prediction is based is correct, then we would observe such contracts. If the theory or my application of it is incorrect, nothing is lost; consumers would simply demand (in the sense of being willing to pay for) other contractual terms. The beauty of a contractual solution, like the beauty of any free contract, is that the parties themselves decide which terms they want.

Many scholars (for example, Richard A. Epstein, George L. Priest, Peter W. Huber, Alan Schwartz, Clark C. Havighurst, and Jeffrey O'Connell) agree with this suggestion. Some prominent scholars in the economics and law tradition, however (William Landes and Richard Posner, and Steven Shavell), have argued that contracts should not be used in product liability relationships. They base their argument on the difficulty that consumers would have in understanding risks involved with products. This is odd since the rest of their analysis rests on assumptions, common in economics, that consumers can make complex calculations in using products. The assumption is that consumers can correctly judge risks in *driving* a car but not in *buying* a car. Moreover, since the arguments advanced here are limited to damage payments, many of the points made by Landes and Posner and by Shavell are irrelevant, since their specific arguments deal with liability rules.

The key to the argument is that consumers would not be willing to pay the expected cost of damage payments for nonpecuniary losses. We observe, for example, that no consumer voluntarily purchases insurance for this type of loss. Consumers would prefer to have more money under conditions when the accident had not occured than when it had. The technical analysis relies on differences between shifts in utility functions and movements along a given utility function. In simple terms, some losses cannot be replaced by money, and consumers would not be willing to pay the fair price for insurance covering such losses.

Although consumers would not want nonpecuniary damage payments as compensation, some theorists argue that this level of damage payments is needed to provide efficient deterrence. This would be true, however, only if there were no other forces for deterrence in the economy. This assumption is not correct. Direct regulation is one force for deterrence. Moreover, firms that provide insufficient levels of safety lose large amounts of valuable reputation capital. Thus, tort law is only one force for safety. It is incorrect to argue that it must carry the entire burden alone. Moreover, it is somewhat anomalous that economists who justify the current state of tort law do so on the basis of deterrence, while those originally advocating this law base their arguments on compensation, a rationale rejected by virtually all economists who have studied the issue.

While current tort law is inefficient, there is a real possibility for changes in tort law leading to much more inefficiency. Some courts have assessed damages based on a theory of hedonic damages, derived from calculations of willingness to pay, which would raise the average level of damages in wrongful death cases by about ten times. The Supreme Court has recently ruled that in one type of matter such damages might be acceptable, in that these damages are not "punitive." If this theory of damages is actually adopted, then the harm caused by tort law would greatly increase. Moreover, even in its current form, tort law, by raising prices for risk-reducing products and services (such as physician care and medicine), may actually lead to increased, rather than reduced, risk. This result is much more likely if the theory of hedonic damages becomes widely used.

While most commentators believe that the courts would refuse to enforce a contract specifying types of damage in tort litigation, there has not been a legal test of this hypothesis. Courts have refused to enforce contracts exculpating injurers of all liability, but there is no evidence regarding a contract such as that proposed here. If such a contract were written and litigated, arguments such as those advanced in this book could be used to demonstrate that the contract was based on rational consumer behavior, not on unequal bargaining power, and therefore should be enforced. Moreover, many state legislatures have written statutes capping tort damages in some cases. The proposal here is much less intrusive than a legislative cap, since it allows parties to choose for themselves the level of damages that they would prefer. Those in favor of legislation allowing free contracting for damage payments might find it useful, in advocating such legislation, to use the arguments explained here.

Many observers believe that a major flaw in twentieth-century law has been the unwillingness of the courts to enforce contracts voluntarily entered into by informed parties. This is clearly a major cause of problems with our current tort system. Allowing parties to specify potential damage payments by contract would be a simple but powerful tool toward returning to a sensible product liability system.

Bibliography

Ashford, Nicholas A., and Robert F. Stone. 1991. "Liability, Innovation and Safety in the Chemical Industry." In *The Liability Maze*, edited by Peter W. Huber and Robert E. Litan. Washington, D.C.: Brookings Institution.

Association of Trial Lawyers of America. N.d. *ATLA in Brief.* Washington, D.C.: ATLA.

Bell, Peter A. 1990. "Analyzing Tort Law: The Flawed Promise of Neocontract." *Minnesota Law Review* 74, pp. 1177–1249.

Blackmon, Glenn, and Richard Zeckhauser. 1991. "State Tort Reform Legislation." In *Tort Law and the Public Interest*, edited by Peter Schuck. New York: W. W. Norton.

Bodine, Larry. 1992. "Hedonic Damages Catch On." *National Law Journal*, March 9, pp. 27–28.

Borenstein, Severin, and Martin B. Zimmerman. 1988. "Market Incentives for Safe Commercial Airline Operation." *American Economic Review* 78: 913–35.

Bovberg, Randall R., Frank A. Sloan, and James F. Blumstein. 1989. "Valuing Life and Limb in Tort: Scheduling 'Pain and Suffering.'" *Northwestern University Law Review* 83: 908.

Brown, John P. 1973. "Toward an Economic Theory of Liability." *Journal of Legal Studies* 2: 323–49.

Calfee, John, and Paul Rubin. 1992. "Some Implications of Damage Payments for Nonpecuniary Losses." *Journal of Legal Studies* 21: 371–411.

Chase, Marilyn. 1992. "Consumer Crusader Sidney Wolfe, M.D., Causes Pain to the FDA, AMA and the Health Industry." *Wall Street Journal*, April 7, p. A18.

Cohen, Jon. 1992. "Is Liability Slowing AIDS Vaccines?" *Science* 256 (April 10): 168–70.

Coleman, Jules L. 1989. "A Market Approach to Products Liability Reform." St. Louis: Center for the Study of American Business, Washington University.

Comanor, William S. 1986. "The Political Economy of the Pharmaceutical Industry." *Journal of Economic Literature* 24: 1178–1217.

Cook, Philip, and Daniel Graham. 1977. "The Demand for Insurance and Protection: The Case of Irreplaceable Commodities." *Quarterly Journal of Economics* 91: 143.

Cooter, Robert D., and Daniel L. Rubinfeld. 1989. "Economic Analysis of Legal Disputes and Their Resolution." *Journal of Economic Literature* 27: 1067.

Cooter, Robert D., and Stephen D. Sugarman. 1988. "A Regulated Market in Unmatured Tort Claims: Tort Reform by Contract." In *New Directions in Liability Law*, edited by Walter Olson. New York: Academy of Political Science.

Cooter, Robert D., and Thomas Ulen. 1988. *Law and Economics*. Glenview, Ill.: Scott, Foresman and Co.

Council on Competitiveness. 1991. "Agenda for Civil Justice Reform in America." Washington, D.C.: Government Printing Office.

Crandall, Robert W. 1991. "Comment." In *The Liability Maze*, edited by Peter W. Huber and Robert E. Litan. Washington, D.C.: Brookings Institution.

Croley, Stephen P., and Jon D. Hanson. 1991. "What Liability Crisis: An Alternative Explanation for Recent Events in Products Liability." *Yale Journal on Regulation* 8: 1–112.

Crouch, Richard, and Edmund Wilson. 1982. *Risk/Benefit Analysis*. Cambridge, Mass.: Ballinger.

"Customizing Liability Rules in the Federal Employees Health Benefits Program." 1986. *Law and Contemporary Problems* 49: 223–41.

Danzon, Patricia. 1984. "Tort Reform and the Role of Government in Private Insurance Markets." *Journal of Legal Studies* 13: 517–50.

———. 1985. "Liability and Liability Insurance for Medical Malpractice." *Journal of Health Economics* 4: 309–31.

Dickens, William T. 1990. "Assuming the Can Opener: Hedonic Estimates and the Value of Life." *Journal of Forensic Economics* 3: 51–60.

Dungworth, Terence. 1988. *Product Liability and the Business Sector: Litigation Trends in Federal Courts*. Santa Monica, Calif.: Institute for Civil Justice, RAND Corp.

Epps, Charles. 1989. "The District Is Driving Its Doctors Away." *Washington Post*, January 29, p. D8.

Epstein, Richard A. 1984. "The Legal and Insurance Dynamics of Mass Tort Litigation." *Journal of Legal Studies* 13: 475–506.

———. 1985. "Products Liability as an Insurance Market." *Journal of Legal Studies* 14: 645–70.

———. 1986. "Medical Malpractice, Imperfect Information, and the Contractual Foundation for Medical Services." *Law and Contemporary Problems* 49: 201–12.

———. 1987. "Legal Liability for Medical Innovation." *Cardozo Law Review* 8: 1139–59.

Ginsburg, William H., Steven J. Kahn, Michael C. Thornhill, and Steven C. Gambardella. 1986. "Contractual Revisions to Medical Malpractice Liability." *Law and Contemporary Problems* 49: 253–64.

Graham, Daniel, and Ellen Pierce. 1984. "Contingent Damages for Products Liability." *Journal of Legal Studies* 13: 441–68.

Graham, John D. 1991. "Product Liability and Motor Vehicle Safety." In *The Liability Maze*, edited by Peter W. Huber and Robert E. Litan. Washington, D.C.: Brookings Institution.

Haddock, David, and Christopher Curran. 1985. "An Economic Theory of Comparative Negligence." *Journal of Legal Studies* 14: 49–72.

Havrilesky, Thomas. 1990. "Valuing Life in the Courts: An Overview." *Journal of Forensic Economics* 3: 71–74.

Havighurst, Clark C. 1986. "Private Reform of Tort-Law Dogma: Market Opportunities and Legal Obstacles." *Law and Contemporary Problems* 49: 143–72.

Henderson, James A., and Aaron D. Twerski. 1987. *Products Liability*. Boston: Little, Brown.

Henderson, James A., and Aaron D. Twerski. 1991A. "Closing the American Products Liability Frontier: The Rejection of Liability without Fault." *New York University Law Review* 66: 1263–1331.

Henderson, James A., and Aaron D. Twerski. 1991B. "Stargazing: The Future of American Products Liability Law." *New York University Law Review* 66: 1332–43.

Hoffer, George E., Stephen W. Pruitt, and Robert J. Reilly. 1988. "The Impact of Product Recalls on the Wealth of Sellers: A Reexamination." *Journal of Political Economy* 96: 663–70.

Huber, Peter W. 1985. "Safety and the Second Best: The Hazards of Public Risk Management in the Courts." *Columbia Law Review* 85: 277–337.

————. 1988. *Liability: The Legal Revolution and Its Consequences.* New York: Basic Books.

Kazman, Sam. 1991. "Death by Regulation." *Regulation* (Fall): 18–22.

Keenan, Donald, and Paul H. Rubin. 1988. "Shadow Interest Groups and Safety Regulation." *International Review of Law and Economics* 8: 21–36.

Kitch, Edmund W. 1985. "Vaccines and Product Liability: A Case of Contagious Litigation." *Regulation* (May/June): 11–18.

Kovacic, William E. 1991. "Reagan's Judicial Appointees and Antitrust in the 1990s." *Fordham Law Review* 60: 49–124.

Landes, William, and Richard Posner. 1975. "The Independent Judiciary in an Interest Group Perspective." *Journal of Law and Economics* 18: 875.

————. 1987. *The Economic Structure of Tort Law.* Cambridge: Harvard University Press.

Larsen, Kim D. 1984. "Strict Products Liability and the Risk-Utility Test for Design Defect: An Economic Analysis." *Columbia Law Review* 84: 2045.

Lasagna, Louis. 1991. "The Chilling Effect of Product Liability on New Drug Development." In *The Liability Maze*, edited by Peter W. Huber and Robert E. Litan, 334–59. Washington, D.C.: Brookings Institution.

Mehlman, Maxwell J. 1990. "Fiduciary Contracting: Limitations on Bargaining between Patients and Health Care Providers." *University of Pittsburgh Law Review* 51: 365–417.

Miller, Ted R. 1989. "Willingness to Pay Comes of Age: Will the System Survive?" *Northwestern University Law Review* 83: 876–907.

————. 1990. "The Plausible Range for the Value of Life—Red Herrings among the Mackerel." *Journal of Forensic Economics* 3: 17–40.

Mitchell, Mark. 1989: "The Impact of External Parties on Brand-Name Capital: The 1982 Tylenol Poisonings and Subsequent Cases." *Economic Inquiry* 27: 601–18.

Mitchell, Mark L., and Michael T. Maloney. 1989. "Crisis in the Cockpit? The Role of Market Forces in Promoting Air Travel Safety" *Journal of Law and Economics* 32: 329–56.

Moore, Michael J., and W. Kip Viscusi. 1990. *Compensation Mechanisms for Job Risks: Wages, Workers' Compensation and Product Liability.* Princeton: Princeton University Press.

National Safety Council. 1986, 1989. "Accident Facts."

Nazario, Sonia L. 1988. "Life and Death: High Infant Mortality Is a

Persistent Blotch on Health Care in U.S." *Wall Street Journal*, November 19: p. 1.

Niehaus, Greg, and Edward A. Snyder. 1992. "Damage Schedules and Their Potential in Mitigating Adverse Selection in the Products Liability System." Chicago: Center for the Study of the Economy and the State, University of Chicago.

O'Connell, Jeffrey. 1981. "A Proposal to Abolish Defendants' Payment for Pain and Suffering in Return for Payment of Claimants' Attorneys' Fees." *University of Illinois Law Review* 1981, 333–69.

———. 1990. "A Model Bill Allowing Choice between Auto Insurance Payable with and without Regard to Fault." *Ohio State Law Journal* 51: 947–83.

Olson, Walter. 1988. "Overdeterrence and the Problem of Comparative Risk." In *New Directions in Liability Law*, edited by Walter Olson. New York: Academy of Political Science.

Peltzman, Sam. 1973. "An Evaluation of Consumer Protection Legislation: The 1962 Drug Amendments." *Journal of Political Economy* 81: 1049.

Peltzman, Sam, and Gregg Jarrell. 1985. "The Impact of Product Recalls on the Wealth of Sellers." *Journal of Political Economy* 93: 512–36.

Posner, Richard A. 1992. *Economic Analysis of Law*. 4th ed. Boston: Little, Brown.

Priest, George. 1981. "A Theory of the Consumer Product Warranty." *Yale Law Journal* 90: 1297.

———. 1985. "The Invention of Enterprise Liability: A Critical History of the Intellectual Foundations of Modern Tort Law." *Journal of Legal Studies* 14: 461–528.

———. 1987. "The Current Insurance Crisis and Modern Tort Law." *Yale Law Journal* 96: 1521.

———. 1988. "Understanding the Liability Crisis." In *New Directions in Liability Law*, edited by Walter Olson, 196–211. New York: Academy of Political Science.

———. 1992. "Can Absolute Manufacturer Liability Be Defended?" *Yale Journal on Regulation* 9: 237–63.

Rea, Samuel A. 1982. "Nonpecuniary Loss and Breach of Contract." *Journal of Legal Studies* 11: 35–54.

Reiser, Stanley Joel. 1991. "Malpractice, Patient Safety, and the Ethical and Scientific Foundations of Medicine." In *The Liability Maze*, edited by Peter W. Huber and Robert E. Litan, 227–50. Washington, D.C.: Brookings Institution.

89

Ringleb, Al H., and Steven N. Wiggins. 1990. "Liability and Large-Scale, Long-Term Hazards." *Journal of Political Economy* 98: 574–95.

Rodgers, Gregory, and Paul H. Rubin. 1989. "Cost Benefit Analysis of All Terrain Vehicles at the CPSC." *Risk Analysis* 9: 63–169.

Rubin, Paul H. 1982. "Common Law and Statute Law." *Journal of Legal Studies* 11: 205–24.

———. 1983. *Business Firms and the Common Law*. Praeger.

———. 1987. "The Dangers of Overstating Safety Risks." *Wall Street Journal* (October 8): 30.

———. 1989. "The Pitfalls of Hedonic Value Use." *National Law Journal* (January 16): 15–16.

———. 1990. *Managing Business Transactions*. New York: Free Press.

———. 1992. Review of Viscusi, *Reforming Products Liability*. *Cato Journal* 11: 332–35.

Rubin, Paul H., and Martin J. Bailey. 1992. "A Positive Theory of Legal Change." Law and Economics Working Paper, Emory University.

Rubin, Paul H., and John E. Calfee. 1992. "Consequences of Damage Awards for Hedonic and Other Nonpecuniary Losses." *Journal of Forensic Economics* 5: 249–60.

Rubin, Paul H., R. Dennis Murphy, and Gregg Jarrell. 1988. "Risky Products, Risky Stocks." *Regulation* 1: 35–39.

Schwartz, Alan. 1988. "Proposals for Products Liability Reform: A Theoretical Synthesis." *Yale Law Review* 97: 353–419.

Shavell, Steven. 1980. "Strict Liability versus Negligence." *Journal of Legal Studies* 9: 1–25.

———. 1987. *The Economics of Accident Law*. Cambridge: Harvard University Press.

Smith, Stan V. 1990. "Hedonic Damages in the Courtroom Setting—A Bridge over Troubled Waters." *Journal of Forensic Economics* 3: 41–50.

Sowle, Kathryn Dix. 1991. "Toward a Synthesis of Product Liability Principles: Schwartz's Model and the Cost-Minimization Alternative." *University of Miami Law Review* 46: 1–111.

Spence, A. Michael. 1977. "Consumer Misperceptions, Product Failure and Producer Liability." *Review of Economic Studies* 44: 561–72.

Stigler, George J., ed. 1988. *Chicago Studies in Political Economy*. Chicago: University of Chicago Press.

Tancredi, Lawrence, and Dorothy Nelkin. 1991. "Medical Malpractice and Its Effect on Innovation." In *The Liability Maze*, edited by Peter W.

Huber and Robert E. Litan, 251–73. Washington, D.C.: Brookings Institution.

Viscusi, W. Kip. 1990. "The Value of Life: Has Voodoo Economics Come to the Courts?" *Journal of Forensic Economics* 3: 1–16.

———. 1991. *Reforming Products Liability*. Cambridge: Harvard University Press.

Viscusi, W. Kip, and William N. Evans. 1990. "Utility Functions That Depend on Health Status: Estimates and Economic Implications." *American Economic Review* 80: 353–74.

Viscusi, W. Kip, and Joni Hersch. 1990. "The Market Response to Product Safety Litigation." *Journal of Regulatory Economics* 2: 215–30.

Weicher, John C. 1984. "The Market for Housing Quality." In *Empirical Approaches to Consumer Protection Economics*, edited by Pauline M. Ippolito and David T. Scheffman, 39–66. Washington, D.C.: Federal Trade Commission.

Wiggins, Steven N., and Al H. Ringleb. 1992. "Adverse Selection and Long Term Hazards." *Journal of Legal Studies* 21: 189–216.

Zuckerman, Stephen, Randall R. Bovberg, and Frank Sloan. 1990. "Effects of Tort Reforms and Other Factors on Medical Malpractice Insurance Premiums." *Inquiry* 27: 167–82.

D. Gale Johnson
Eliakim Hastings Moore
  Distinguished Service Professor
  of Economics Emeritus
University of Chicago

William M. Landes
Clifton R. Musser Professor of
  Economics
University of Chicago Law School

Glenn C. Loury
Department of Economics
Boston University

Sam Peltzman
Sears Roebuck Professor of Economics
  and Financial Services
University of Chicago
  Graduate School of Business

Nelson W. Polsby
Professor of Political Science
University of California at Berkeley

Murray L. Weidenbaum
Mallinckrodt Distinguished
  University Professor
Washington University

Research Staff

Leon Aron
Resident Scholar

Claude E. Barfield
Resident Scholar; Director, Science
  and Technology Policy Studies

Walter Berns
Adjunct Scholar

Douglas J. Besharov
Resident Scholar

Jagdish Bhagwati
Visiting Scholar

Robert H. Bork
John M. Olin Scholar in Legal Studies

Dinesh D'Souza
John M. Olin Research Fellow

Nicholas N. Eberstadt
Visiting Scholar

Mark Falcoff
Resident Scholar

Gerald R. Ford
Distinguished Fellow

Murray F. Foss
Visiting Scholar

Suzanne Garment
Resident Scholar

Patrick Glynn
Resident Scholar

Robert A. Goldwin
Resident Scholar

Gottfried Haberler
Resident Scholar

Robert W. Hahn
Resident Scholar

Robert B. Helms
Resident Scholar

Karlyn H. Keene
Resident Fellow; Editor,
  The American Enterprise

Jeane J. Kirkpatrick
Senior Fellow; Director, Foreign and
  Defense Policy Studies

Marvin H. Kosters
Resident Scholar; Director,
  Economic Policy Studies

Irving Kristol
John M. Olin Distinguished Fellow

Michael A. Ledeen
Resident Scholar

Susan Lee
DeWitt Wallace–Reader's Digest
  Fellow in Communications
  in a Free Society

Robert A. Licht
Resident Scholar; Director,
  Constitution Project

Chong-Pin Lin
Resident Scholar; Associate Director,
  China Studies Program

John H. Makin
Resident Scholar; Director, Fiscal
  Policy Studies

Allan H. Meltzer
Visiting Scholar

Joshua Muravchik
Resident Scholar

Charles Murray
Bradley Fellow

Michael Novak
George F. Jewett Scholar in Religion,
  Philosophy, and Public Policy;
  Director, Social and
  Political Studies

Norman J. Ornstein
Resident Scholar

Richard N. Perle
Resident Fellow

Thomas W. Robinson
Resident Scholar; Director, China
  Studies Program

William Schneider
Resident Fellow

Bill Shew
Visiting Scholar

J. Gregory Sidak
Resident Scholar

Herbert Stein
Senior Fellow

Irwin M. Stelzer
Resident Scholar; Director, Regulatory
  Policy Studies

Edward Styles
Director of Publications

W. Allen Wallis
Resident Scholar

Ben J. Wattenberg
Senior Fellow

Carolyn L. Weaver
Resident Scholar; Director, Social
  Security and Pension Studies